CENTRAL

NORTH

SOUTH & EAST

WEST

GREENWICH

AROUND

ACROSS

TOP FIVES

LONDON
UNLOCKED

by
Emily Kerr, Joshua Perry
and
Tessa Girvan

illustrations by
Katherine Hardy

NOTES

This book belongs to:

CENTRAL

NORTH

SOUTH & EAST

WEST

GREENWICH

AROUND

ACROSS

TOP 5s

CONTENTS

CENTRAL

NORTH

SOUTH & EAST

WEST

GREENWICH

AROUND

ACROSS

TOP FIVES

POLICE STATION

MAP OF LONDON

Luton

Stanstead

Heathrow

City

KEY

Parks

The Thames

Gatwick

CENTRAL
NORTH
SOUTH & EAST
WEST
GREENWICH
AROUND
ACROSS
TOP FIVES

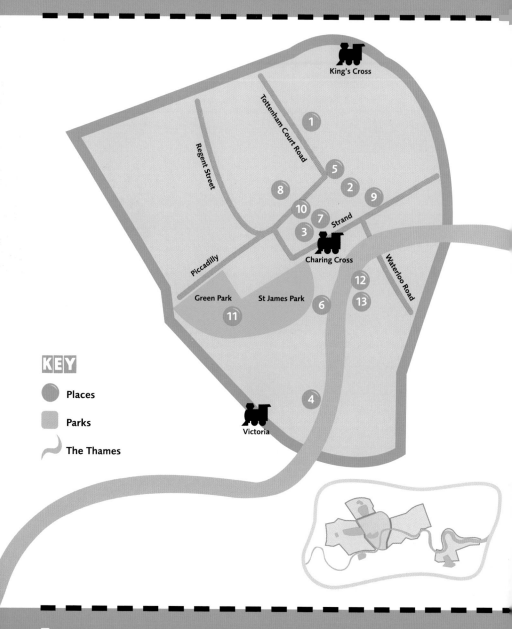

KEY

⬤ Places

▢ Parks

〜 The Thames

CENTRAL

NORTH

SOUTH & EAST

WEST

GREENWICH

AROUND

ACROSS

TOP FIVES

SEE A MUMMY UNWRAPPED

...at the British Museum

Like everyone, the British Museum loves its mummy. However, in this case we're talking about *3,000 year old Egyptian mummies.*

Mummies were made by removing a dead person's insides, wrapping the corpse in linen and gooey resin, then putting it in a fancy coffin. Opening a mummy's coffin can cause damage, so it's rare to catch a glimpse of one. But the museum has got round this by exhibiting several mummies in different states of unwrap. There are also some mummified cats, and even a falcon.

Sticker Scores

5 — PERFECT PYRAMID

4 — TERRIFIC TOMB

3 — COMMON CASKET

2 — CURSED COFFIN

1 — I WANT MY *MUMMY*

Best of the Rest

Have a historic sleepover.
Members of the museum's Young
Friends Club get to stay over after
dark and explore the exhibits. You
have to be eight years old or more to
take part.

Top Tip

The Samsung Digital Discovery
Centre holds family workshops every
weekend where you can learn how to
use the latest digital equipment
and software. See the website
for listings.

**How do you
make a mummy
dance?**

Play it some
wrap music!

← The British Museum's Great Court

Fascinating Facts

★ **The name mummy comes from the
Arabic word mummia, which means
tar. The Arabs who first saw the tombs
called the bodies this because they
were covered in black sticky stuff.**

★ Egyptian embalmers used special tools
to remove a body's internal organs. To
get the brain out they would stick a hook
in through the corpse's nostrils, as if they
were picking its nose. It is not known if
they then ate the bogeys!

★ **The museum is home to the 2,500
year old Elgin Marbles – sculptures of
Greek gods and other mythological
figures. There's controversy over
whether they should actually be there.
The Greeks think they were taken
illegally and want them returned to
Athens.**

PLAN YOUR VISIT ①

British Museum
Great Russell Street, WC1B 3DG
www.britishmuseum.org

📞 **020 7323 8000**

🕐 **Daily 10.30-17.30**

⊖ **Holborn / Tottenham Court Road**

FREE ✕ 🎁 ☂

I want to go here ☐

DRIVE A TUBE TRAIN

...at the London Transport Museum

Public transport in London has changed a lot over the last 200 years. There have been trains, trams, taxis, trolleybuses, the tube – and even some forms of transport that don't begin with a t!

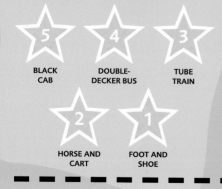

The London Transport Museum has real, life-sized, original vehicles. There are around 25 models on display, many of which you can get inside. The highlight has to be the tube-train simulator. You can climb into a realistic carriage, and then work the controls to make the train travel between stations. Video screens replace the windows so that it really looks like you're moving. *Mind the gap!*

Sticker Scores

⭐ 5	⭐ 4	⭐ 3
BLACK CAB	DOUBLE-DECKER BUS	TUBE TRAIN

⭐ 2	⭐ 1
HORSE AND CART	FOOT AND SHOE

Best of the Rest

🔑 Try on drivers' uniforms in the Interchange Gallery, an interactive space that's just for kids.

🔑 Play detective on the Stamper Trail. There are thirteen stamper posts hidden throughout the museum – see if you can find them all!

Photo Op
Get someone to snap you sitting in your favourite old vehicle or pretending to drive it.

← What London transport used to look like!

Fascinating Facts

⭐ **London's bus network is one of the largest city networks in the world – it has about 7,000 buses operating on around 700 routes.**

⭐ Before engines were invented, buses and taxis were pulled along by horses. Almost 1,000 tonnes of horse dung was dropped on the streets of London every day. It would take you 14,000 years to do that much poo!

⭐ **London taxi drivers spend between two and four years passing the 'Knowledge', which involves learning in detail all the streets within a six mile radius of Charing Cross. Research has shown this can make a driver's brain bigger!**

 **PLAN YOUR VISIT** 2

London Transport Museum
39 Wellington St, Covent Garden, WC2E 7BB
www.ltmuseum.co.uk

📞 **020 7379 6344**

🕐 **Sat-Thu 10.00-18.00, Fri 11.00-18.00**

⊖ **Covent Garden**

££ ✗ 🎁 ☂

I want to go here ☐

FIND THE WORLD'S SMALLEST POLICE

...in Trafalgar Square

Barely big enough for one policeman, the world's smallest police station is located inside a lamppost on Trafalgar Square in Central London.

It was originally built as a lookout post so police (or one of them at least) could keep a close eye on any riots and demonstrations that took place in the square. It contained a direct telephone line to the police headquarters at Scotland Yard, so reinforcements could be swiftly summoned when needed. Nowadays the tiny police station is used as a storage cupboard by cleaners!

How do pigeons tell the time?

With a *coo-coo* clock!

Sticker Scores

5
STAR
SUPERINTENDENT

4
IMPORTANT
INSPECTOR

3
SENIOR
SERGEANT

2
COMPETENT
CONSTABLE

1
BUNGLING
BURGLAR

POLICE STATION

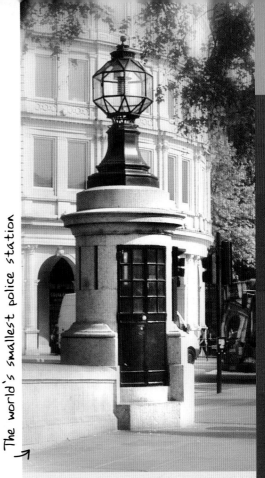

STATION

Fascinating Facts

⭐ **Trafalgar Square has its very own police hawk! The square's resident pigeons can cause damage and pester tourists, so the hawk is under orders to fly around and scare away any troublesome customers.**

⭐ In 1843, fourteen builders had a full three-course dinner sitting on top of Nelson's Column. History doesn't tell us how or where they used the toilet!

⭐ **The central point of London is in Trafalgar Square. It's under the statue of Charles I. All distances on signs are measured from this point.**

⭐ On the inside of Admiralty Arch (south-west of Trafalgar Square) you'll find a carved nose, one metre above adult head height. It was stuck on by an artist called Rick Buckley in 1997. Goodness *nose* why he did it!

The world's smallest police station ↗

Photo Op
Lounge like a lion beside Nelson's Column! Look at the lions at the bottom of the column and copy their pose. *Roaarrr!*

PLAN YOUR VISIT ③

Trafalgar Square
Trafalgar Square, WC2
www.london.gov.uk/trafalgarsquare
⊖ **Charing Cross**
FREE ✗

I want to go here ☐

CREATE YOUR OWN ART

...at Tate Britain

Even grown-ups know that art galleries can be a bit boring. There are just so many random historical pictures to look at: Fat King, Naked Woman, Horse, Fat King. . . .

Thankfully, Tate Britain is one of the good galleries, with British art on display from the year 1500 right up to the present day. You don't have to be an art expert to enjoy it. Play detective and try finding the oldest, the newest, the largest and the smallest paintings in the collection.

Look out for Liminal, the gallery's daily family sculpture workshop. You can interact with works of art, and also have a go at building and crafting. It's great to create at the Tate!

Sticker Scores

5 MARVELLOUS MASTERPIECE

4 PERFECT PAINTING

3 SATISFYING SCULPTURE

2 DUBIOUS DRAWING

1 SCRUFFY SKETCH

Best of the Rest

🔑 Travel from Tate to Tate. There's a brilliant boat service between Tate Britain and its sister gallery, Tate Modern. Boats run every 40 minutes during museum opening hours, and it's a terrific way to see the Thames. Tate Modern has an Open Studio with art materials (open on weekends only), as well as an Interactive Zone with hands-on games.

← Half-boy, half-cardboard robot

Top Tip
Check out the Tate Kids website. It has games, arty tips and even a gallery to upload your own crafty creations.

Fascinating Facts

⭐ **Every year Tate Britain hosts the Turner prize, a controversial modern art competition. Previous entries have included a pickled shark, a dirty bed and a painting done with elephant poo – *ugh*!**

⭐ Just up the road from Tate Britain is the MI5 headquarters, where British spies work. If you're walking to the gallery from Westminster you'll go past the building, called Thames House, just after Lambeth Bridge.

Why was the painting sent to prison?
Because it had been *framed!*

PLAN YOUR VISIT ④

Tate Britain
Millbank, SW1P 4RG
www.tate.org.uk

📞 020 7887 8888

🕐 Sat-Thu 10.00-18.00
Fri 10.00-22.00

⊖ Pimlico

FREE 🍴 🎁 ☂

I want to go here ☐

WATCH STREET PERFORMERS

...in Covent Garden

If you're a famous entertainer it's easy to arrange a theatre tour. But what do you do if you're a talented performer and nobody knows your name? Well, one option is to head to Covent Garden . . .

Street performing, or busking, is one of the oldest forms of entertainment. It's also the way that many famous acts have started out. Cirque du Soleil, former James Bond actor Pierce Brosnan, and musician Bob Dylan all spent time busking.

Covent Garden is home to many weird and wonderful performers, including opera singers, acrobats, magicians and people pretending to be statues. All of them hope you'll like them enough to throw them a bit of money.

Sticker Scores

⭐ 5
FANTASTIC FIRE-EATERS

⭐ 4
TERRIFIC TUMBLERS

⭐ 3
AGILE ACROBATS

⭐ 2
POOR PUPPETEERS

⭐ 1
SAD STATUES

Best of the Rest

 Search for a souvenir in the market. There are lots of shops in the covered arcade as well, including a Disney Store and a Build-A-Bear Workshop.

 Marvel at maps at Stanfords in nearby Long Acre. It's the world's largest map and travel bookshop and has been going for over 150 years. There's also a nice café where you can rest your weary feet.

 Pack a picnic and head to nearby Neal's Yard, a tiny triangular courtyard with small benches you can sit on while you munch your lunch.

← Look, no hands!

Fascinating Facts

★ **Covent Garden is the only area of London with a formal licence for street entertainment. Performers have to audition in front of the square's management before they're allowed to hit the streets. Think of it as London's own version of *X Factor*.**

Photo Op

Somewhere around Covent Garden you'll usually find someone pretending to be a statue. Search for one, then copy their pose. Just be careful not to include them in the picture unless you're happy to throw them some money. Even statues get angry if they think they are being ignored!

PLAN YOUR VISIT (5)

Covent Garden Market
Covent Garden, WC2E
www.coventgardenlondonuk.com
⊖ Covent Garden
`FREE`

I want to go here ☐

HEAR BIG BEN'S BONGS

...at Westminster Palace

Big Ben is the name people give to the giant clock tower attached to the Houses of Parliament. However, originally Big Ben was really the nickname of the big, bongtastic bell inside the tower.

The building is officially called St Stephen's Tower and is one of the most famous sights in London. Despite being over 150 years old, the clock is incredibly reliable. The main bell rings every hour on the hour, and four smaller bells chime every fifteen minutes. For the best bonging experience listen at midday so you can hear twelve bongs in a row.

Sticker Scores

5 — ATOMIC CLOCK
4 — QUARTZ WATCH
3 — STOPWATCH

2 — SUNDIAL

1 — EGG TIMER

Fascinating Facts

★ **In 1949 Big Ben was delayed by four and a half minutes when a big flock of starlings perched on the minute hand of the clock. The weight of the birds stopped the hand from turning. Unfortunately, blaming the starlings is unlikely to work when you're late for a maths lesson!**

★ The secret to the clock's top timekeeping lies in a stack of old penny coins that sits on top of its pendulum. The pennies adjust the weight of the pendulum, affecting the speed at which it swings. Adding or removing one penny alters the time by 0.4 seconds a day.

★ **The bell weighs around fourteen tonnes. That means it's as heavy as 165,000 starlings (but much less likely to fly away).**

★ The UK's first traffic light was put up close to Big Ben, in 1868. This was to allow MPs to cross the road safely.

Bongtastic Big Ben

Photo Op
If you get the angles right you can take a photo which makes it look like you're leaning against Big Ben. Stand with the tower in the background and hold your hand out so that from the camera's viewpoint it looks like Big Ben is supporting your weight.

PLAN YOUR VISIT 6

Big Ben
The Palace of Westminster, Westminster, SW1A 0AA

www.parliament.uk/bigben

⊖ Westminster

FREE

I want to go here ☐

MAKE A BRASS RUBBING

...at St Martin-in-the-Fields

Sadly, this kind of brass rubbing is unlikely to conjure up a genie! It's actually a form of art developed hundreds of years ago.

Memorial brasses were popular between the years 1200 and 1600 and were often found in churches. They usually featured important people or religious figures. Think of them as a bit like memorials, gravestones and art all rolled into one.

St Martin-in-the-Fields church has a brilliant Brass Rubbing Centre where you can have a go at making one yourself. Put a piece of paper on top of a brass stencil and brush coloured crayons over it. It may take some time to perfect your technique, but stick with it and you could make a *brass*-terpiece!

Sticker Scores

5 GLORIOUS GOLD

4 SHIMMERY SILVER

3 COOL COPPER

2 BASIC BRASS

1 TINFOIL

Fascinating Facts

⭐ There are only around 8,000 brasses left in England, and very few anywhere else in the world. There used to be more in Europe, but they were mostly melted down so that the brass could be used to make armour, weapons and even jewellery.

⭐ St Martin's is the official parish church of the royal family, which means you never know when a prince or princess might pop in to sing a hymn or two!

Why was the lamp brassed off?
Because it had been *rubbed up* the wrong way!

Top Tip

St Martin-in-the-Fields has a family friendly café in its crypt, just next to the Brass Rubbing Centre. The crypt used to be a burial room, and gravestones still line the floor. So, if you like the idea of having a snack while surrounded by ghosts, this is the place to do it!

Making a brass rubbing

PLAN YOUR VISIT ⑦

St Martin-in-the-Fields
Trafalgar Square, WC2N 4JJ
www.stmartin-in-the-fields.org

📞 020 7766 1100

🕐 Mon-Wed 10.00-18.00
Thu-Sat 10.00-20.00, Sun 11.30-17.00

⊖ Charing Cross

£ 🍴 🎁 ☂

I want to go here ☐

CHECK OUT CHINATOWN

...in central London

Several areas of London are linked to a particular country. Brick Lane is a Bangladeshi cultural centre, for example, and South Kensington has a very French feel. But the part best known for its foreign influence is Chinatown.

London's first Chinatown began in Limehouse, east London, after Chinese sailors moved to the city in the 1700s. However, much of it was destroyed during World War Two bombings. So a new site was established in Soho, where it remains today.

Chinatown has grown into a big community full of restaurants, herbal medicine stores and reflexology specialists. You can see all of this by taking a short walk through the bustling streets. Keep an eye out for the dramatic red gates at each entrance.

Sticker Scores

5 — GREAT WALL OF CHINA

4 — CHINESE TAKEAWAY

3 — CHINESE FORTUNE COOKIE

2 — CHINESE LANTERN

1 — CHINESE BURN

Best of the Rest

 Find fabulous fancy dress, face paint and costumes, at Angels - an amazing costume store near Chinatown (119 Shaftesbury Avenue).

 Saunter over to Seven Dials in Covent Garden. It's a small roundabout where seven roads meet. At the centre is a statue surrounded by sundials facing in all directions. There used to be a pub on every corner, but now it's just a nice place to visit.

← Roaarrr!

Top Tip

Chinatown is best seen during one of its big festivals. Chinese New Year, which falls on a different day in either January or February every year, is the highlight. Several hundred thousand people head to Chinatown to watch the parades, decorations and street performers. Check the website for more details.

Photo Op

The Chinese zodiac is made up of twelve animals all with different personalities. It's a bit like star signs, but linked to the *year* you were born in, not the month. Find out what animal you are and then take a photo of you posing as that creature.

PLAN YOUR VISIT 8

Chinatown

Gerrard Street, W1D

www.chinatownlondon.org

⊖ **Leicester Square / Picadilly Circus**

FREE

I want to go here ☐

ICE-SKATE IN AN EIGHTEENTH-CENTURY,

...at Somerset House Ice Rink

In the 1600s it was so cold in London that people held frost fairs on the ice-covered Thames. The river no longer freezes over, but during the winter you can still ice-skate if you know where to go.

Somerset House is the site of London's first outdoor ice rink. It opened in 2000 and operates day and night between November and January in the building's beautiful eighteenth-century courtyard. Don't worry if you've never skated before; there is a Penguin Club where you can learn how.

Somerset House has been many things throughout the years including a palace, an army building and a tax office, but in our opinion it's most fun when it's frozen!

Why shouldn't you tell a joke whilst you're ice skating? Because the ice might *crack up!*

Sticker Scores

5 ICE CREAM	4 ICE LOLLY	3 ICE CUBE
2 ICE AGE	1 *I-SCREAM*	

COURTYARD

Similar Spots

🔑 The locations of London's outdoor ice rinks change each year, but previously they have been in the following places:

- Hyde Park (centre)
- Natural History Museum (south)
- Tower of London (east)
- Canary Wharf (east)
- Kew Gardens (south west)

Check online to confirm if they're running and to book tickets.

← Having an ice time in the Penguin Club!

Top Tip

Remember to wear two pairs of socks and take some gloves with you. Ice is, unsurprisingly, quite cold!

Fascinating Facts

⭐ **The oldest ice skates ever were found in Sweden and are from the ninth century A.D. They were made from bones (hopefully from dead animals, not dead people!) strapped to the bottom of shoes.**

⭐ The world speed record for skating on ice is 32 miles per hour, and was set in Canada in 2000. That's fast enough to break the speed limit on most London roads.

⭐ **The Netherlands is home to a 200 kilometre skating race. It's only been held fifteen times because the ice has to be thick enough to not break and this doesn't always happen. Falling through the ice would be *snow* joke.**

PLAN YOUR VISIT 9

Somerset House Ice Rink

The Strand, WC2R 1LA

www.somersethouse.org.uk

📞 020 7845 4600

🕐 Daily (winter) 10.00-23.30

⊖ Temple

££

I want to go here ☐

CATCH A MUSICAL

...in the West End

Over ten million people see a musical in London every year. Tourists love the grand theatres, elaborate costumes and tunes that are catchier than chickenpox.

There are around 50 theatres in the West End (the area around Covent Garden) and they put on musicals and plays throughout the year. Successful shows last for decades, whereas rubbish ones can be cancelled after just one day. If you see one you like, the chances are you'll be singing the songs in the shower for months afterwards!

Sticker Scores

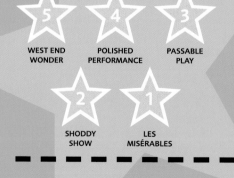

5 WEST END WONDER

4 POLISHED PERFORMANCE

3 PASSABLE PLAY

2 SHODDY SHOW

1 LES MISÉRABLES

Fascinating Facts

⭐ *The Mousetrap* by Agatha Christie is the longest continually running play in the world. The first show was in 1952. In total it has been performed 20,000 times (though not with the same cast!).

⭐ The shortest ever run at a West End theatre didn't even last until the end of the first performance. *The Intimate Revue*, staged in 1930, was so long and complicated that the actors were forced to cut the final scenes. It wasn't shown a second time!

The Lion King at the Lyceum

Top Tip
You can often get half-price tickets for performances on the same day at the TKTS booth in Leicester Square. Each morning at 10.00, theatres send over lists of their leftover seats. Be careful you go to the right place – TKTS is the only official ticket booth on the square.

Photo Op
Pretend to be an actor and strike a dramatic pose in front of a West End theatre.

PLAN YOUR VISIT

See www.londontheatre.co.uk for theatre listings and locations

🕐 Times vary by performance

⊖ Leicester Square (most performances)

£££ ☂

I want to go here ☐

MARCH WITH SOLDIERS

...outside Buckingham Palace

Lots of important people have bodyguards. But the Queen is the only person in the country to have her very own selection of soldiers.

The Queen's Guard is made up of soldiers with big guns and furry hats. Their job is to protect the Queen when she's at home. They take it in turns to guard her, and the ceremony where they swap over is called the Changing of the Guard.

There are several good places to watch the Changing of the Guard. Start at Horse Guards Arch at 11.00, where you can see the cavalry (soldiers on horseback) change over. Then dash to Wellington Barracks on Birdcage Walk and watch the band play as the new guard gets ready. Finally, march alongside the changing soldiers as they head towards Buckingham Palace.

Sticker Scores

5 — QUEEN'S GUARD

4 — BODYGUARD

3 — SECURITY GUARD

2 — LIFE GUARD

1 — MOUTH GUARD

Best of the Rest

🔑 Visit The Guards Museum on nearby Birdcage Walk (a great option if it's raining outside!). You can try on a bearskin hat, and it's free to get in if you're under sixteen.

🔑 Bring some bird-seed and feed the ducks in the lake in St James's Park, which is next to the palace.

Top Tip
The Changing of the Guard doesn't take place every day (and it can be postponed if it's raining), so check online for timings before you visit.

← "Aargh, I can't see where I'm going!"

Fascinating Facts

⭐ There are five different infantry regiments in the Queen's Guard: Grenadier Guards, Coldstream Guards, Scots Guards, Irish Guards and Welsh Guards. Each regiment has its own uniform.

⭐ Henry VIII designed St James's Park as a private playground for the royal family. When James I came to the throne he stocked it with exotic animals, including camels, crocodiles and even an elephant! So the public were probably happy that it was surrounded by a high brick wall!

Photo Op
Have your picture taken next to a member of the Queen's Guard. There's one standing on his own near St James's Palace.

PLAN YOUR VISIT 11

Changing of the Guard
Buckingham Palace, Horse Guards Arch and Wellington Barracks, SW1

www.changing-the-guard.com (unofficial website)

🕐 **Selected days 11.00**

⊖ **Charing Cross for Horse Guards Arch, Victoria for Buckingham Palace**

FREE

I want to go here ☐

SEE SHARKS SWIM BENEATH YOUR

...at the Sea Life London Aquarium

There's something very *fishy* about London's Aquarium. And it's not the tuna sandwiches in your packed lunch!

An aquarium is a living land of fish, full of tanks containing different species. Sea Life is cleverly arranged so you can walk through, under and above the fish, turtles, seahorses and octopuses. The best bit is the Shark Walk. A glass walkway stands above a shoal of sixteen fabulous finned friends which swim beneath your feet as you move along. There's also an interactive Shark Academy, where you can learn all about these super sea creatures and even touch shark skin. It's *fin*-omenal!

Sticker Scores

⭐ 5	⭐ 4	⭐ 3
GREAT WHITE SHARK	HAMMERHEAD SHARK	WHALE SHARK
⭐ 2	⭐ 1	
REEF SHARK	GOLDFISH	

What do you call a fish with no eyes?

Fsh!

FEET

Fascinating Facts

⭐ Scientists can tell the age of a shark or a fish by counting the rings that form in its ear bones. The technique is a bit like the way you can tell a tree's age by counting the rings in its trunk. Mind you, trees are less likely to bite!

⭐ Americans are 30 times more likely to be killed by aeroplane parts falling from the sky than be killed by a shark. Unless they're swimming in a shark-infested swimming pool, of course.

Best of the Rest

🔑 Watch Gentoo penguins play in the penguin ice cave. Sea Life London has the only colony of Gentoos in the country. The curious creatures have wide white stripes across the top of their heads and long, stiff tail feathers.

Hmm, I wonder if that's a red herring?

Top Tip

Book online in advance to avoid the really big queues that can form outside the aquarium. While you're on the Internet you can also check out the feeding times of the sharks and fish.

PLAN YOUR VISIT 12

Sea Life London Aquarium
County Hall, Westminster Bridge Rd, SE1 7PB
www.visitsealife.com/London

📞 **0871 663 1678**

🕐 **Mon-Thu 10.00-18.00**
Fri-Sun 10.00-19.00

⊖ **Westminster / Waterloo**

£££ 🎁 ☂

I want to go here ☐

PLAY I-SPY IN THE SKY

...on the London Eye

Everyone loves a game of I-spy, but it's best when there's lots to see. So there's no better place to play than the **London Eye**, where you can check out some of London's finest views.

The London Eye is also known as the Millennium Wheel, because it opened to the public on the last day of 1999 to celebrate the new millennium. It's a gigantic observation wheel, which lifts you off the ground and takes you around a giant loop in the sky.

The views from the Eye are spectacular – on a clear day you can see as far as Windsor Castle, which is 25 miles away! You could try spying Big Ben, St Paul's Cathedral or Buckingham Palace as they're all visible during your journey.

Sticker Scores

5 BIG WHEEL

4 ENTICING EYE

3 FAIR FERRIS

2 RUBBISH RIDE

1 *WHEELY DISAPPOINTING*

Fascinating Facts

⭐ There are 32 glass passenger capsules on the London Eye. Each capsule weighs ten tonnes, which is the same as over one million pound coins (but less likely to make you a millionaire!).

⭐ The London Eye measures 135 metres from top to bottom, which is taller (but less gruesome) than a stack of 5,500 real eyes.

⭐ The wheel spins at approximately 0.6 miles per hour, or twice the speed of a tortoise. That means that your journey lasts around 30 minutes – plenty of time for several games of I-spy.

I spy with my little eye something beginning with . . .

Make A Day Of It

🔑 Gawp at the biggest cinema screen in the UK, at the BFI IMAX. It covers the same amount of space as 1,000 widescreen televisions! You watch the films through a special pair of glasses, to get a thrilling 3-D effect. **www.bfi.org.uk**

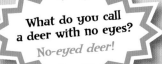

What do you call a deer with no eyes?
No-eyed deer!

PLAN YOUR VISIT 13

The Merlin Entertainments London Eye

County Hall, Westminster Bridge Road, SE1 7PB
www.londoneye.com

📞 0871 781 3000

🕐 Daily (summer) 10.00-21.00
Daily (out of season) 10.00-20.30
Opening hours can vary during school holidays

⊖ Westminster / Waterloo

£££ ✗ 🎁

I want to go here ☐

35

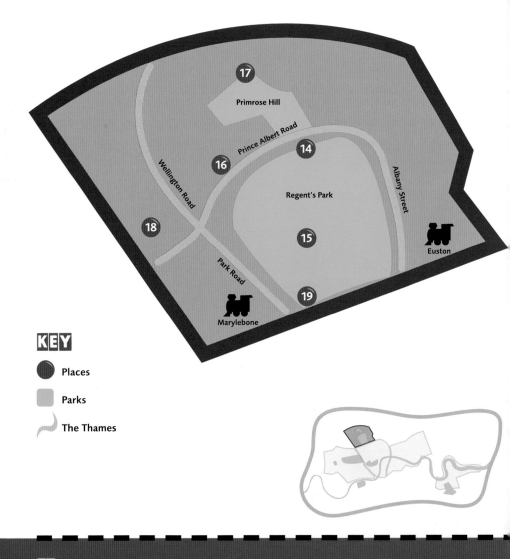

17 Primrose Hill

Prince Albert Road

16

14

Wellington Road

Regent's Park

Albany Street

18

15

Park Road

Euston

19

Marylebone

KEY

● Places

▮ Parks

〰 The Thames

CENTRAL

NORTH

SOUTH & EAST

WEST

GREENWICH

AROUND

ACROSS

TOP FIVES

WATCH PENGUINS BEING FED

...at ZSL London Zoo

London Zoo is home to over 750 different species. And, as animals can't cook, they all need feeding. You can watch many of the animals being fed, but the peckish penguins are particularly popular.

ZSL London Zoo is located in the city's Regents Park. It's the world's oldest scientific zoo, which means that it was originally used by scientists to study species. You'll see all kinds of animals   including gentle giraffes, giant Galapagos tortoises and mysterious moon jellyfish. Londoners are lucky that they still have a zoo – it nearly closed down in 1991 but thankfully public support kept it open.

Try and watch the patient penguins at dinner time. They line up in an orderly queue, waiting to be fed. It's a s-*peck*-tacular sight!

Sticker Scores

5 PERFECT PENGUINS

4 GREAT GORILLAS

3 BRILLIANT BIRDS

2 REASONABLE REPTILES

1 PUNY PLANKTON

Best of the Rest

🔑 Explore underground tunnels in the Animal Adventure part of the zoo. You can also splash in the water zone and traipse through tree tops.

🔑 Admire butterflies from around the world in the caterpillar-shaped Butterfly Paradise.

🔑 Discover a dragon in the Komodo Dragon House. These large lizards are highly intelligent (though sadly they aren't much use in helping you with your homework!).

← Single file, please!

What do penguins eat for lunch?
Ice berg-ers!

Fascinating Facts

⭐ **Penguins eat up to one kilogram of fish each day, and they swallow each fish in a single gulp (we do the same with chocolate cake!).**

⭐ Many animals have funny names to describe a group of them. For example, you would say a pride of lions, a tower of giraffes, or a crash of rhinoceroses. A collection of penguins is usually called a colony.

⭐ **When a flea jumps, it accelerates twenty times faster than a space rocket. Sadly, scientists have not yet found a way to take advantage of this – if you strap a shuttle onto a flea's back you're unlikely to end up on the moon.**

PLAN YOUR VISIT 14

ZSL London Zoo
Outer Circle, Regent's Park, NW1 4RY
www.zsl.org

📞 0844 225 1826

🕐 **Daily (summer) 10.00-17.30
Closes earlier out of season**

⊖ **Camden Town / St. John's Wood**

£££ 🍴 🎁

I want to go here ☐

HIRE A PEDALO

...in Regent's Park

Rowing boats are fun, but they can be quite tiring for the person doing all the work. Pedalos, on the other hand, are ideal for leisurely larking about on a lake.

A pedalo is a bit like a cross between a bike and a boat – you push the pedals with your legs and a paddle wheel spins around to move you through the water. You can also steer using a rudder to make sure you're going in the right direction.

Sticker Scores

5 OUTSTANDING OCEAN

4 SUPERB SEA

3 GREAT LAKE

2 LAUGHABLE LAGOON

1 PATHETIC POND

Regent's Park has two pedalo places. There's a lake for children's pedalos only, but you can also hire a bigger pedalo or a rowing boat on the main lake if you are with an energetic adult.

Best of the Rest

🔑 Watch a children's play, or check out one of the regular puppet shows, at Regent's Park's awesome outdoor theatre. Shows run throughout the summer months.

🔑 Let off some steam at the Hanover Gate playground. There's a play sculpture, water play and tree house area.

🔑 Catch a concert at the park's bandstand, east of the boating lake. There are frequent performances in the summer.

🔑 Find the giant newt in the Wildlife Garden, near the York Gate entrance. The eight metre-long sculpture is made of earth, turf and wild flower plugs.

The boating lake at Regent's Park

Photo Op

If someone you're with stays on dry land while you head out in your pedalo, get them to take a pic of you 'doing a doughnut'. This is the name for spinning around in a small circle. Push the rudder hard to the right or left and peddle as fast as you can – you'll make a doughnut shape in the water!

PLAN YOUR VISIT 15

The Boathouse Café
Hanover Gate, Regent's Park, NW1 4NU
www.royalparks.org.uk/parks/regents_park

📞 **020 7724 4069**

🕐 **Boats available from 10.00, times vary by month, weather permitting**

⊖ Baker Street

£

I want to go here ☐

CRUISE ON A CANAL BOAT

...on Regent's Canal

Regent's Canal has been in use for nearly 200 years. Like other canals it was built to transport cargo, but as we now have trains and lorries, today it's mostly used for cool cruises.

Canals were a marvel of the Industrial Revolution, when an entire network was built across the UK. Before then goods were lugged about on horse-drawn carts.

These days many canals are still maintained as tourist attractions. In London, several companies operate canal-boat tours from Little Venice to Camden. The journey takes about an hour and a half and you get to travel through the damp and mysterious Maida Hill tunnel.

Sticker Scores

5 CRACKING CANAL

4 WONDERFUL WATERWAY

3 REASONABLE RIVER

2 SIMPLE STREAM

1 PIFFLING PUDDLE

Fascinating Facts

★ Narrowboats are often painted with elaborate designs. Two of the most common ones are roses and castles. No one seems to know why!

★ In some parts of London people still live on canal boats, as they're often cheaper (and cooler) than houses. Around 15,000 people live on canals around the UK.

★ London has its very own museum of canal boats, near Kings Cross. Bizarrely, it is also a museum of ice cream! In the days before freezers were invented ice had to be imported from Norway, and it travelled part of the way by canal.

↖ Home, sweet home!

Top Tip

The London Waterbus Company lets you combine your canal cruise with a visit to London Zoo (p38). It has a special canalside entrance gate which allows you to skip the zoo's queues.

PLAN YOUR VISIT 16

London Waterbus Company

Various other companies also operate – check online for more information

www.londonwaterbus.co.uk

📞 020 7482 2550

🕐 Daily (summer) 10.00-17.00
Shorter hours out of season

⊖ Warwick Avenue / Camden Town
(depends where you want to start!)

££

I want to go here ☐

FLY A KITE

...on Primrose Hill

Primrose Hill is an ideal spot for kite flying. Unsurprisingly, given the name, it's hilly, which means it's often quite windy. So all you need to do is climb to the top and get flying!

Primrose Hill is popular for lots of reasons. Dog walkers go there for the open space, tourists love it for the amazing views of London, and posh people like the smart surrounding area. The hill is also perfect for sledging in winter, and occasionally people even try to ski down, though we definitely do not recommend you try this yourself. Instead, let your kite take flight – just make sure you don't get carried off in a big gust of wind!

Sticker Scores

5 GINORMOUS GALE

4 POWERFUL WIND

3 GLORIOUS GUSTS

2 STEADY BREEZE

1 WEEDY WAFTS

Similar Spots

🔑 Kite Hill on Hampstead Heath is, unsurprisingly, another great place for kite flying.

🔑 Check out 'Top five places to run around' on p164 for other good London parks where you can fly your kite.

← Hold on tight to your kite!

Photo Op

Get someone to take a photo of you looking as if you are being carried up in to the air by your kite. Make sure the string is tight and then jump up in the air to make it look as if you're being pulled off the ground. But do remember to let go if you actually find yourself being lifted up!

Fascinating Facts

⭐ The record for the largest number of kites flown on a single line is 11,284. The record is held by a Japanese kite maker. Nice going!

⭐ It is thought that the first kites were flown over 3,000 years ago – 1,000 years before paper existed. They were made from leaves.

⭐ The highest recorded altitude for a train of kites is 9,740 metres above sea level, which is even higher than Mount Everest. It happened in Germany in 1919 with eight kites attached to the same string.

PLAN YOUR VISIT 17

Primrose Hill
Primrose Hill Road, Camden, NW3 3NA
www.primrosehill.com
⊖ Chalk Farm
FREE

I want to go here ☐

SEE THE OLDEST PRIZE IN CRICKET

...at Lord's Cricket Ground

When a football team wins the Premier League they get a shiny silver trophy. But the cricket authorities find that sort of thing a bit too showy. So the biggest prize in the sport is a tiny terracotta urn full of ashes. Woo-hoo!

The Ashes is the name for the on-going Test series played since 1882 between England and Australia. Although the teams are supposedly playing for the Ashes urn, the winner doesn't get to keep it. Instead it's always on display at Lord's Cricket Ground, the 'Home of Cricket'.

You can tour the ground and see the Ashes. During the tour you'll also get to see the players' dressing rooms, the futuristic media centre and the MCC cricket museum. You'll be *bowled* over!

Sticker Scores

5	4	3
FAST BOWLER	SERIOUS SPINNER	MEDIUM SWINGER

2	1
UNDERARM CHUCKER	BALL DROPPER

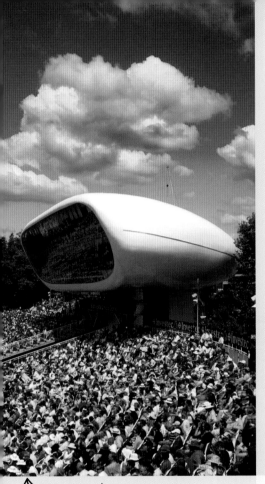

The Lord's media centre

Fascinating Facts

⭐ In 1882 after Australia beat England on home soil for the first time, a newspaper published a story saying that English cricket was dead, the body was being cremated and the ashes would go to Australia. The next season when England went to Australia, the media said they were off to regain the ashes. An Australian woman then gave the English captain an urn supposedly containing the ashes of cricket stumps, and 'The Ashes' was born.

⭐ In 1936, during a game at Lord's, Jahangir Khan bowled a ball that hit a sparrow on the way to the batsman. The sparrow died instantly and fell against the stumps. Its stuffed body is now preserved in the museum.

What is an insect's favourite sport?
Cricket!

Photo Op
Get a snap of yourself pretending to be a journalist in the media centre. Look at the camera and shout "England win the Ashes!"

PLAN YOUR VISIT 18

Marylebone Cricket Club
Lord's Cricket Ground
St John's Wood, NW8 8QN
www.lords.org

📞 **020 7616 8595**

🕐 **Tour times vary –**
check the website for details

⊖ **St John's Wood**

££ 🍴 🎁

I want to go here ☐

MEET BECKS AND BEYONCÉ

...at Madame Tussauds

Have you ever wanted to meet your heroes? Well, at Madame Tussauds you can. Just so long as you don't mind them being made of wax!

Madame Marie Tussaud was a wax modeller from France. She opened her museum containing creepily accurate wax copies of famous people in London in 1835. Back then she focused on well-known leaders and explorers, whereas nowadays you'll find everyone from sports stars to royals to rock idols.

David Beckham and Beyoncé are two of the most popular exhibits, but if they don't excite you there are hundreds of others to choose from. OK, so they might not be the *real* stars, but they do make for great photos!

Sticker Scores

5 HOLLYWOOD HERO

4 ROCK LEGEND

3 SOAP STAR

2 X FACTOR CONTESTANT

1 BIG BROTHER WANNABE

Best of the Rest

🔑 Take a terrific track through London's history on the Spirit of London ride. You'll see Shakespeare write, watch the Great Fire of 1666 and experience the swinging 60s.

🔑 Have your photo taken with the Queen on the Royal Balcony.

← Which one's the wax figure?

Top Tip
The attraction is very popular and there's often a long wait to get in, so get there early if you can!

Fascinating Facts

⭐ **During the French Revolution, Madame Tussaud searched through the corpses of people whose heads had been chopped off and made wax masks from her favourites. This is not a hobby we would recommend.**

⭐ Each wax figure takes about four months to make and costs around £150,000. That's enough to buy 300,000 Mars bars (or one mid-range Ferrari).

Photo Op
You won't need any help taking fun photos at Madame Tussauds – every wax figure is a potential super-snap!

PLAN YOUR VISIT 19

Madame Tussauds
Marylebone Road, NW1 5LR
www.madametussauds.com

📞 **0871 894 3000**

🕐 **Daily 09.30-17.30**
(opens extended hours at peak times)

⊖ **Baker Street**

£££ 🍴 🎁 ☂

I want to go here ☐

The image depicts a wax figure owned and created by Madame Tussauds

49

SOUTH & EAST LONDON

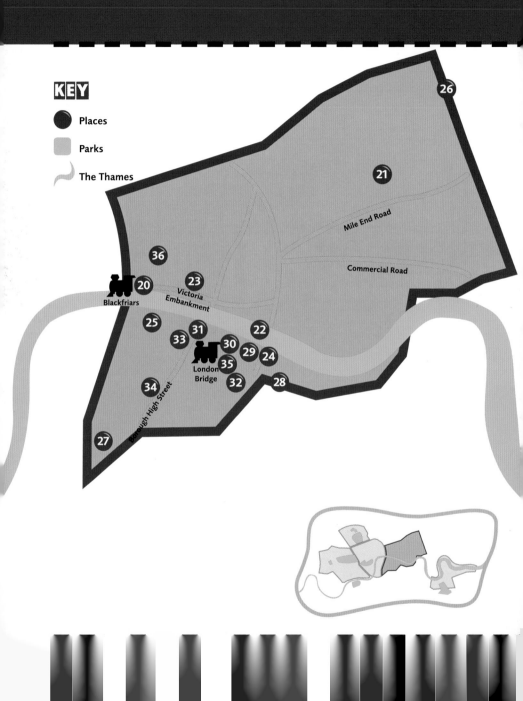

KEY

Places

Parks

The Thames

26

21

Mile End Road

Commercial Road

36

20
Blackfriars

23
Victoria
Embankment

25

31

33

22

30

29

24

35

London
Bridge

32

28

34

Borough High Street

27

CENTRAL

NORTH

SOUTH & EAST

WEST

GREENWICH

AROUND

ACROSS

TOP FIVES

WALK AROUND A WHISPERING GALLERY

...at St Paul's Cathedral

Have you ever wanted to be able to hear a whisper on the other side of a room just like some of your teachers? Well, now you can, by visiting the whispering gallery at St Paul's Cathedral.

The cathedral was built after the Great Fire of London in 1666. It's best known for its big dome, which was inspired by the Catholic Church of St Peter in Rome. This was controversial, since being Catholic in England was generally discouraged at this time and often led to you being burned to death! Inside the dome, you can climb up a spiral staircase to reach the whispering gallery. Its perfectly round shape means you can hear someone whispering over on the other side of the room. So be careful what you say!

Sticker Scores

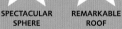

5 DELIGHTFUL DOME

4 SPECTACULAR SPHERE

3 REMARKABLE ROOF

2 CURVY CEILING

1 LEAKY TENT

Best of the Rest

🔑 Get a 360 degree view across London from the Golden Gallery at the top of the dome.

🔑 Search for the tombs of famous people. Good ones to look out for include the graves of Horatio Nelson, Florence Nightingale and the architect of St Paul's Cathedral, Sir Christopher Wren.

> Why are tombs always unwell?
> Because they keep coffin!

Fascinating Facts

⭐ **On Sir Christopher Wren's tomb it says in Latin:** *Reader, if you seek his monument, look around you.* **In other words:** *Check out my cathedral. Cool, huh? I betcha I'll be remembered for this . . .*

⭐ The dome measures 108 metres from top to bottom. That's taller than 140 penguins standing on top of each other (but less likely to topple over!).

⭐ **For years, only towns that had a cathedral in them were granted the status of city. To get an upgrade these days, towns simply need to have a few hundred thousand residents and ask the Queen nicely.**

PLAN YOUR VISIT 20

St Paul's Cathedral
St Paul's Churchyard, EC4M 8AD
www.stpauls.co.uk

📞 020 7236 4128

🕐 **Mon-Sat 08.30-16.00**
Closed for special services

⊖ St Paul's

££ ✕ 🎁 ☂

I want to go here ☐

PUT ON A PUPPET SHOW

...at the Museum of Childhood

Adults have loads of boring museums designed for them. So it's only fair that the Museum of Childhood just contains exhibits dedicated specifically to kids' stuff.

The Museum of Childhood, in Bethnal Green, contains toys, clothes and games for children past and present. One highlight is Art Smarts, a daily workshop where you can come up with your own artistic creations. We suggest you plump for the particularly popular puppet-making option. Once you've made your personalised puppets you can put on a real show in the museum's puppet theatres. Check the website for workshop timings.

Sticker Scores

5 PERFECT PUPPET

4 MARVELLOUS MARIONETTE

3 DESIGNER DOLL

2 CARDBOARD CUT-OUT

1 SMELLY SOCK

Best of the Rest

🔑 See a seventeeth-century-doll's house. The museum owns the largest public collection of doll's houses in the UK. Some of them originally belonged to members of the royal family!

🔑 Make a robot come to life in the Moving Toys Gallery. You'll learn all about moving playthings, from toy trains to rocking horses, and there are lots of interactive features.

🔑 Get crafty in the Creativity Gallery, where you can come up with where you can come up with your own ideas for art, plays and creative design. Oh, and you can also push your face into a giant wall of nails. Trust us; it's more fun than it sounds!

← Moving images from the days before cinema

Fascinating Facts

⭐ **Over one billion Barbie dolls have been sold since they were launched in 1959. If all the Barbie dolls ever manufactured were laid end to end, they would circle the Earth three and a half times.**

⭐ Robots were first dreamt up by a Czech author called Karel Čapek, who wrote a play about a factory that made artificial people. He called them robots because the word *robota* in Czech means work.

Photo Op
Take a photo with Robbie the Robot in the Moving Toy Gallery. If you stand in front of him, it looks like he's stretching out his arms to give you a hug.

PLAN YOUR VISIT 21

V&A Museum of Childhood
Cambridge Heath Road, Bethnal Green, E2 9PA
www.museumofchildhood.org.uk

📞 020 8983 5200

🕐 Daily 10.00-17.45

⊖ Bethnal Green

FREE 🍴 🎁 ☂

I want to go here ☐

CHECK OUT THE CROWN JEWELS

...at the Tower of London

Most people store their jewellery in a box. The royal family go several steps further. They keep theirs in a box, in a house, in a tower, surrounded by a moat and guarded by soldiers *and* birds!

The Crown Jewels are kept safely under lock and key (and behind thick glass) in the Tower of London's Jewel House. They've been there for over 700 years, and are only taken out when they're needed by kings and queens for special royal events. As well as a selection of crowns, you'll also see orbs (round balls) sceptres (long sticks) and swords. But be warned; only royals can get away with a sword as an accessory for their party outfit!

Sticker Scores

5 DIAMOND CROWN

4 JEWELLED SCEPTRE

3 GOLDEN SWORD

2 ORDINARY ORB

1 PLASTIC BRACELET

Best of the Rest

🔑 Take a guided tour of the Tower and find out about the people who were tortured and executed there. Your guide will be one of the Beefeaters (the guardians of the Tower).

🔑 Try on old style armour and weapons inside the White Tower Armoury.

🔑 Pretend to be a soldier defending the tower as you walk along the battlements to the fortress exhibition.

Photo Op
Snap yourself posing with a Beefeater in full costume.

← Beefeaters guarding the Crown Jewels

Fascinating Facts

⭐ **Officially, the guardians of the Tower are called the Yeoman Warders, but people usually just call them Beefeaters. Their nickname is thought to have come from the fact that the guards used to receive part of their pay in meat rations.**

⭐ There are always 35 Beefeaters guarding the Tower. A new Beefeater is only ever appointed when an existing one retires or dies.

⭐ **Prisoners who were beheaded at the Tower actually had to pay for their own execution. It is not known whether the guards' favourite inmates were given a special discount!**

PLAN YOUR VISIT 22

Tower of London
Tower Hill, EC3N
www.hrp.org.uk/TowerOfLondon

📞 0844 482 7777

🕐 Tue-Sat 09.00-16.30,
Sun-Mon 10.00-16.30

⊖ Tower Hill

£££ ✗ 🎁

I want to go here ☐

CLIMB 311 STEPS

...to the top of the Monument

If you've ever run up a flight of stairs, you'll know that it's a pretty exhausting thing to do. So imagine how you'll feel after traipsing up the 311 steps that lead to the top of London's Monument!

The Monument is a tall, thin column that was built in 1677 to commemorate the Great Fire of London (p80). The top part is a flaming golden urn, which represents the fire. It was designed by Sir Christopher Wren, who was also responsible for nearby St. Paul's Cathedral (p52).

Climb up the Monument and you'll be rewarded with amazing views all across London. And you will definitely deserve second helpings at dinner time after all that exercise!

Sticker Scores

5 MASSIVE MONUMENT

4 GIANT BEANSTALK

3 FIREMAN'S LIFT

2 LONG LADDER

1 PORCH STEPS

Fascinating Facts

★ **Six people have fallen to their death from the top of the Monument. In the 1840s, an iron cage was installed on top and thankfully there haven't been any since!**

★ The Monument is 61 metres tall – the height of a twenty-storey building. That makes it the tallest stone column in the world.

★ **The Monument was originally built to be used as a scientific observatory. The urn covers a central shaft which once held a telescope, and there is also an underground laboratory for measuring gravity.**

How many steps did you say?

Photo Op
Try taking overlapping pictures of the view all the way around the top of the monument. You can then get them printed and lay them out side by side for an incredible 360 degree collage!

PLAN YOUR VISIT 23

Monument
Junction of Monument Street and Fish Street Hill, EC3

www.themonument.info

📞 **0207 626 2717**

🕐 **Daily 09.30-17.30**

⊖ Monument

£

I want to go here ☐

TOWER ABOVE THE THAMES

...on Tower Bridge

Most bridges are designed to provide a single river crossing. Tower Bridge's architects decided to go one better – they designed a magnificent double-decker structure instead.

Tower Bridge is one of London's most recognisable landmarks. Famously, the bridge splits in two: both sides of the road bridge swing upwards until they are almost vertical, so that boats can glide through.

It's free to cross the lower level as a pedestrian, but you can also pay to go up to the top. The views are amazing – though viewing is restricted for smaller visitors, so only taller travellers will want to part with their pennies.

Sticker Scores

5 BEAUTIFUL BRIDGE

4 CRACKING CROSSING

3 WORTHWHILE WALKWAY

2 STEPPING STONES

1 JUST JUMP

Fascinating Facts

⭐ Tower Bridge's design was finally agreed in 1884 after much debate. Over 50 designs were looked at before the judges finally selected one that was submitted by, umm, one of the judges.

⭐ In 1952 a number 78 double-decker bus driver was surprised to find Tower Bridge opening as he drove across. He had no time to stop, but was smart enough to accelerate. As a result the bus was going fast enough to clear the metre gap that had opened up between the two parts of the bridge.

⭐ Honourable Londoners are sometimes offered the title Freeman. One of the benefits of this position is the right to drive sheep over Tower Bridge. These days people rarely bother since you'd be *baaa*-king mad to keep sheep in London!

Not a good time to drive across

Top Tip
The bridge website has a list of all the planned bridge lift times over the coming months. Use them to arrange your visit at a time when you'll see it open and close.

Photo Op
Just to the northeast of the bridge there is a statue of a girl and a dolphin. It's a spectacular spot for a photo of Tower Bridge.

PLAN YOUR VISIT 24

Tower Bridge
Tower Bridge Road, SE1 2UP
www.towerbridge.org.uk

📞 020 7403 3761

🕐 Daily (summer) 10.00-18.00
Daily (out of season) 09.30-17.30

⊖ Tower Hill

£ 🍴 🎁 ☂

I want to go here ☐

TAKE A TOUR OF SHAKESPEARE'S

...at Shakespeare's Globe Theatre

William Shakespeare wasn't just the most famous playwright in the world. He was also an actor, and he part-owned a theatre called the Globe.

The Globe was where many of his performances were first aired. The original building was pulled down hundreds of years ago, but in 1997 a faithful reconstruction of the theatre was opened near the same site.

You can take a tour of the theatre, and there's also a great exhibition with replica costumes, musical instruments, special effects and even an ancient printing press, where you can find out what life was like for an actor at the Globe of 1599.

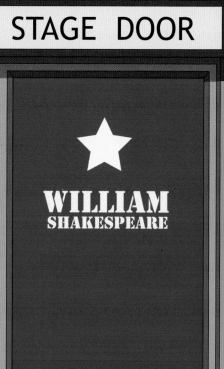

STAGE DOOR

★

WILLIAM SHAKESPEARE

Sticker Scores

5 — OUTSTANDING ACTOR

4 — TALENTED THESPIAN

3 — CONVINCING COMEDIAN

2 — PASSABLE PERFORMER

1 — FORGETTABLE FOOL

THEATRE

Similar Spots

🔑 Many of London's theatres run backstage tours. You often need to book in advance, so check online before you visit. Here are some of the best:

The National Theatre (central) lets you watch the workshops where sets from the shows are created. You can also visit all three auditoriums and the theatre's backstage areas. **www.nationaltheatre.org.uk**

The tour at the Theatre Royal Drury Lane (central) is hosted by three professional actors who play characters from its murky past. **www.reallyuseful.com/theatres/theatre-royal-drury-lane**

The Royal Opera House (central) has a backstage tour that gives you access to its latest equipment during the backstage tour. If you're lucky you may even get the chance to drop in on the Royal Ballet while they're rehearsing. **www.roh.org.uk**

← The gates of the Globe

Fascinating Facts

⭐ **The original Globe burned down in 1613 after a cannon misfired during a performance of Shakespeare's *King Henry VIII*. No one was hurt – except a man whose flaming trousers had to be put out with a bottle of beer! That must have been a bit *ale*-arming.**

⭐ The rebuilt theatre was closed again in 1642, this time following pressure from the Puritans. They were a radical religious group who thought having fun was evil. They shut down all London's theatres, pubs and even banned Christmas. Meanies.

PLAN YOUR VISIT 25

Shakespeare's Globe Theatre
21 New Globe Walk, Bankside, SE1 9DT
www.shakespearesglobe.com

📞 **020 7902 1500**

🕐 **Daily 10.00-17.00, tour times vary**

⊖ **London Bridge / Mansion House**

££ ✗ 🎁

I want to go here ☐

SHOP 'TIL YOU DROP

...at Westfield Stratford City

Westfield Stratford City isn't the sort of place you go just to pick up a pint of milk. It's London's largest shopping centre, and it's a pretty impressive place.

Opened in 2011, Westfield Stratford City is a shiny new shopping centre located next to London's Olympic Park. With 300 stores inside its doors, it's like an all-weather city!

But shops aren't the only thing you'll find at this mega mall. There's also a seventeen-screen cinema showing the latest movies and a 1950s-themed bowling alley called All Star Lanes.

Sticker Scores

5 ENTHRALLING MALL

4 SUPER CENTRE

3 STANDARD STORE

2 BARGAIN BASEMENT

1 SHUT UP SHOP

Start by scoring a strike on one of their fourteen lanes, then head to the restaurant for burgers, milkshakes and cakes. We reckon it'll *bowl* you over!

Similar Spots

Westfield

🔑 Westfield London in Shepherd's Bush is another enormous centre with a similar mix of shops, restaurants and entertainment.

🔑 It's not a mall, but Oxford Street is one of the top clothes shopping destinations in Europe. Check out the huge Topshop, which has loads of high-fashion clothes. Then pop round the corner to trendy Carnaby Street.

Fascinating Facts

⭐ **40,000 tonnes of structural steel was used in the construction of Westfield. That's about the same weight as 62,500 Formula 1 cars (but less nippy around corners!).**

Why did the skeleton go to the shopping centre?
To get to the *Body* Shop!

Best of the Rest

🔑 Peer at the Olympic Park from the viewing area of the John Lewis department store. Look out for the Olympic Stadium, the curved roof of the Aquatic Centre and the Orbit – a 115 metre high observation tower that's made up of twisting, spiralling loops of steel.

PLAN YOUR VISIT 26

Westfield Stratford City
Montfichet Road, Olympic Park, EC20
www.westfield.com/stratfordcity

🕐 **Mon-Fri 10.00-21.00**
   Sat 09.00-21.00
   Sun 11.00-17.00

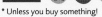

FREE* ✕ 🎁 ☂
* Unless you buy something!

I want to go here ☐

UNCOVER SPIES' SECRETS

...at the Imperial War Museum

Being a spy in wartime is a dangerous job. This was particularly true during World War Two, when Britain's Special Forces played a vital role in protecting the country.

The Imperial War Museum was set up to show people what war is really like. One of the best exhibitions is Horrible Histories: Spies. Based on the bestselling books of the same name, it's all about the exploits of undercover agents during World War Two. The exhibits cover everything from code cracking to cool gadgets and detection-dodging disguises.

Sticker Scores

5 MISSION ACCOMPLISHED

4 COOL CAMOUFLAGE

3 GOOD GADGET

2 DODGY DISGUISE

1 MISSION IMPOSSIBLE

We recommend taking the Stamper Trail, which sets you a special mission to complete. It's the closest you'll come to being a spy without having to change your identity!

↙ The naval guns outside the Imperial War Museum

Best of the Rest

🗝 Marvel at medals. The Lord Ashcroft Gallery has the world's largest collection of Victoria Crosses (medals awarded to soldiers for bravery in battle). The Extraordinary Heroes exhibition tells the stories behind each of the awards.

🗝 Gawp at planes and tanks in the new First World War Galleries (opening Summer 2014).

🗝 Check out the mighty fifteen-inch naval guns at the front of the museum. These were taken from real warships.

Top Tip
The museum is currently undergoing an overhaul and some parts will remain closed until 2014, so check what's open before you travel.

Fascinating Facts

⭐ **World War Two began in 1939, when Britain declared war on Germany. Around fifty million people are thought to have lost their lives in the conflict. Many more were injured.**

⭐ During World War Two, London (along with other British cities) suffered frequent night-time attacks from German bombers. The attacks were known as 'The Blitz,' and they destroyed large areas of the city.

⭐ **Boys turning eighteen in wartime had no choice but to join the army. Conscription was a law which required all men up to the age of 41 to join the military.**

PLAN YOUR VISIT 27

Imperial War Museum
Lambeth Road, SE1 6HZ
www.iwm.org.uk

📞 020 7416 5320

🕐 Check website for opening times

⊖ Elephant & Castle / Lambeth North

FREE 🍴 🎁 ☂

I want to go here ☐

DISCOVER DESIGN

...at the Design Museum

Going to the toilet is normally a necessary but dull part of everyday life. However, at the Design Museum there are snazzy loos which make it a much more e-*loo*-gent experience!

The Design Museum was set up in 1989 and it exhibits all types of design, including advertising, fashion and architecture. They have put lots of effort into making it fun to visit.

Sticker Scores

5
SLICED
BREAD

4
MP3
PLAYER

3
COMPUTER
CONSOLE

2
HULA
HOOP

1
CHOCOLATE
TEAPOT

Don't miss the Design and Make workshops which are held on Sunday afternoons in the riverside studio. There's everything from jewellery design to illustration, so it's a great place to discover your passion for fashion!

↙ Looking around the Design Museum

Similar Spots

🔑 Find out more about fashion at The Fashion and Textile Museum (east). It's located near the Design Museum, so you could combine both in a day trip.
www.ftmlondon.org

🔑 The Victoria and Albert museum (p98) describes itself as 'the world's greatest museum of art and design'.
www.vam.ac.uk

🔑 The Museum of London (p84) contains a wide range of clothing (not a range of wide clothing!) and textiles with links to London's history.
www.museumoflondon.org.uk

Top Tip

Don't forget to pick up a free family trail from the admissions desk. It's has puzzles, pictures and fun activities to do as you make your way through the museum.

Fascinating Facts

⭐ **The building where the Design Museum is based used to be a banana warehouse.**

⭐ Each year the Design Museum awards a Designer of the Year prize. Previous winners include Jonathan Ive, who designed the iPod, and Jamie Hewlett, who created the cartoon music group Gorillaz.

Why did the belt go to jail?
He *held up* a pair of pants!

PLAN YOUR VISIT 28

Design Museum
Shad Thames, SE1 2YD
www.designmuseum.org

📞 020 7403 6933

🕐 Daily 10.00-17.45

🚇 Tower Hill / London Bridge

£ ✕ 🎁 ☂

I want to go here ☐

SCALE A SKYSCRAPER

...at The Shard

The Shard is a super skyscraper that can be seen from all over London. At 310 metres high, it's *S*-hard to miss!

This bumper building houses shops, restaurants and a swanky hotel. But the bit you'll want to visit is the observation area on the 68th - 72nd floors. Thankfully you don't have to take the stairs: there's a super speedy lift that'll get you there in under a minute.

Sticker Scores

5 SKY-SCRAPER	**4** MEGA MONUMENT	**3** BEARABLE BUILDING
2 TERRIBLE TOWER	**1** *BARREL*-SCRAPER	

The most spectacular views are from the outside deck on the 72nd floor. Look down (if you dare!) and see if you can make out the miniature buses, trains and houses below you. The world looks small when you're 72 storeys tall!

Best of the Rest

🔑 Learn about London's landmarks with a touch screen Tell Scope. These high tech telescopes teach you all about the sights you can spot from the Shard.

🔑 Gawp at the Gherkin. Don't worry, we're not suggesting that you peer at a pickle! The Gherkin is the nickname for 30 St Mary's Axe - a curved glass building with a rounded tip on the opposite side of the Thames.

Top Tip
Pre-book your eticket online and print it at home before you visit. That way you won't have to queue to see the view!

← The Shard lit up for opening night

Fascinating Facts

⭐ **The Shard's name comes from its distinctive design. The glass panels that cover the building look like shards (broken fragments) of glass, reaching up towards the sky.**

⭐ The Shard's apartments are some of the priciest pads in London. The 224 metre- high luxury penthouse is valued at around £50 million. Sounds a bit *steep* to us!

⭐ **The world's tallest skyscraper is the Burj Khalifa in Dubai, which stands at half a mile high! That's about the same height as two and half Shards stacked on top of each other (but less likely to take a tumble!).**

PLAN YOUR VISIT 29
The View from the Shard
Joiner Street, London, SE1
www.theviewfromtheshard.com

📞 0844 499 7111

🕐 **Daily 09.00-22.00**

⊖ **London Bridge**

£££ ✗ 🎁

I want to go here ☐

GUIDE A WARSHIP'S GUNS

...on the HMS *Belfast*

Life on the HMS *Belfast* was a bit like being at a boys' boarding school – but without the maths lessons! There were about 950 men on the ship, but unlike boarding school there were big guns and even bigger battles.

HMS *Belfast* was launched in 1938, just in time to play an important role in World War Two. During the war she captured German ships and protected British convoys.

The *Belfast* was finally turned into a museum in 1971 and now you can explore all nine of her decks.

Sticker Scores

5	**4**	**3**
ADMIRAL OF THE FLEET	COMMODORE	COMMANDER
	2	**1**
	LIEUTENANT	STOWAWAY

Head to the gun turret on the ship's bow (the front) where you'll see real ammunition. Then climb up to the Gun Direction Platform at the top of the main tower and gawp at the ginormous guns. Look through the binoculars, take aim and (pretend to) fire!

Fascinating Facts

⭐ Being a crew member on the HMS *Belfast* was a risky business. The ship's doctors used 35.5 miles of bandages on sickly sailors between 1950 and 1952.

⭐ The ship's powerful guns could blast their big bullets up to twelve and a half miles. If they were fired today they would reach as far as Heathrow Airport.

⭐ The *Belfast* didn't escape the war without damage – she was badly hit in 1939 by a detonating magnetic mine as she left the Firth of Forth in Scotland. The impact was so great she was out of service for almost three years.

↖ The humongous HMS Belfast

What's a Sea Monster's favourite food?
Fish and *ships*!

Photo Op
Get a snap of you sitting in the Admiral's Bridge while pointing out to sea.

PLAN YOUR VISIT ㉚
HMS Belfast
Morgan's Lane, Tooley Street, SE1 2JH
www.iwm.org.uk

📞 0207 940 6300

🕐 Daily (summer) 10.00-18.00
Closes earlier out of season

⊖ London Bridge

£ ✗ 🎁

I want to go here ☐

GO MUDLARKING

...on the Thames

Mudlarks were children with one of the worst jobs in history. During the 1700s and 1800s, they would pick through the mud and rubbish of the Thames, searching for anything of value.

An average day would involve them hunting for items among dead people, deceased pets and disgusting poo. And after all that it wasn't even very profitable – mudlarks were lucky to make one penny per day!

Don't worry, we're not suggesting you give up school to pick up poo. These days the Thames is much cleaner, and just a few hours of searching along the shore can reveal ancient artefacts and modern treasures. Of course, you should always go with an adult, and be careful what you pick up.

Sticker Scores

5 — HIDDEN TREASURE

4 — MUDDY MONEY

3 — INTERESTING ARTEFACTS

2 — TATTY TOYS

1 — PILE OF POO

The banks of the Thames

Fascinating Facts

⭐ There were other unpleasant jobs that children used to do in London at around the same time as the mudlarks. Toshers searched for valuables in the sewers and grubbers scavenged in drains.

⭐ There is a massive seven metre difference between the Thames' low and high tide at London Bridge. That's the same as around six poor young mudlarks standing on each other's shoulders.

⭐ Modern mudlarks turn up some pretty exciting treasure. Recent finds have included a medieval purse, an iron dagger and badges worn by pilgrims (religious travellers). The best samples are displayed in the Museum of London (p84).

Top Tip
Check the tide times for the Thames before you go – it's much better to try mudlarking at low tide when there is more of the river bank exposed.

Photo Op
Create a display of everything interesting you've found and take a picture of it. But no poo photos, please!

PLAN YOUR VISIT 31

Mudlarking
The South Bank, near Tate Modern.
Gates in the railings allow you access to the Thames at low tide.

🚇 Southwark / London Bridge

`FREE`

I want to go here ☐

WATCH A PLAY FOR KIDS

...at the Unicorn Theatre

A unicorn is a mysterious, mythical, horse-like creature with a horn. The Unicorn Theatre is, sadly, neither horse-like nor horned, but it does put on great plays!

Unlike other theatres, the Unicorn puts on plays for children only. Originally operating out of an army van, the Unicorn Theatre Company finally got its own building in 2005. Since then, more than 200,000 visitors have been here to see plays, workshops and events.

Each year the Unicorn puts on over 620 performances – so there's plenty for you to choose from. There are also workshops and other activities for families. Check the website for the latest programme.

Sticker Scores

5 THRILLING THEATRE

4 AWESOME AUDITORIUM

3 SATISFACTORY STAGE

2 VARIABLE VENUE

1 LITTLE LIVING ROOM

Fascinating Facts

⭐ The name unicorn was chosen for the theatre because these creatures are said to be exciting figures of legend, which exist only if you believe in them. This is a little bit like plays, which are only fun if you forget that they're not real and go along with the performance.

⭐ The main stars of the *Harry Potter* movies were all aged between eleven and thirteen when the first film was released. Although Daniel Radcliffe, the actor who played Harry, had been on television before, Rupert Grint and Emma Watson (who played Ron Weasley and Hermione Granger) had previously only ever performed in school plays.

The theatre's unicorn statue

Photo Op
In the theatre's main entrance there is a big statue of a unicorn. Get a snap of you posing with it.

PLAN YOUR VISIT 32

Unicorn Theatre
147 Tooley Street, Southwark, SE1 2HZ
www.unicorntheatre.com

📞 **020 7645 0560**

🕐 **Performances during the afternoons & evenings, times vary**

⊖ **Tower Hill / London Bridge**

££ ✖

I want to go here ☐

SLEEP ON A PIRATE SHIP

...at the Golden Hinde

Aarrrr, me hearties! Budding pirates take note: once a month there's a sleepover on a replica Tudor galleon near London Bridge.

The *Golden Hinde* was a ship used by Sir Francis Drake on his round-the-world expedition. Along the way his men attacked and raided any Spanish vessel they came across. They were heroes to the English, but unsurprisingly the Spanish took a different view and called them pirates. Now you can relive the experience: not by robbing a Spanish person, but by sleeping on the *Golden Hinde*. You'll get to dress up as a pirate, try a tasty Tudor dinner and then sleep on the ship's gun deck amongst the cannons.

Sticker Scores

5 **BURIED TREASURE**

4 **GOLDEN BARS**

3 **PIECES OF EIGHT**

2 **COPPER COIN**

1 **EMPTY CHEST**

Fascinating Facts

⭐ Captain Drake was supposed to be looking for good trading spots, and his plans were supported by Queen Elizabeth I. However, along the way he soon realised that piracy would be more profitable, so he changed his focus to attacking Spanish ships instead.

⭐ The original *Golden Hinde*'s round-the-world trip took three years and lasted from 1577 to 1580. This replica ship has sailed the equivalent of more than five times this distance since she was launched in 1973.

⭐ Ships are conventionally referred to as 'she'. This has nothing to do with how long they take putting on their make-up. They are also often given female names – in recent years, the name *Miss Behavin'* has been particularly popular.

Tucking in to a tasty Tudor feast

What did the pirate pay for his peg leg and hook hand?
An arm and a leg!

Top Tip
If you can't stay overnight, why not go on a *Golden Hinde* Pirate Fun Day? You'll be able to fire a cannon and fight with a cutlass! They take place most Saturdays – call for details.

PLAN YOUR VISIT 33

The Golden Hinde
St Mary Overie Dock, Cathedral Street, London, SE1 9DE

www.goldenhinde.com

📞 020 7403 0123

🕙 Daily 10.00-17.30, monthly sleepovers

⊖ London Bridge

£££ (overnight)   ££ (Fun Day)

I want to go here ☐

DRESS UP AS A FIREFIGHTER

...at the London Fire Brigade Museum

Who wouldn't want to be a firefighter? They get the best hats, the coolest trucks and the slidiest poles. However, a few hundred years ago, you might have thought differently . . .

The London Fire Brigade museum is all about the history of firefighting in London, from the Great Fire of London in 1666 right up to the present day. You can look at old engines and the equipment used when it was a lot less fun to be a firefighter. Back then firemen wore hats made of leather, and instead of hosepipes they often relied on volunteers passing buckets of water from hand to hand.

Sticker Scores

5 GREAT FIRE OF LONDON

4 FOREST FIRE

3 CAMPFIRE

2 CANDLE

1 DAMP MATCH

Fortunately, things are a bit more advanced today – you can try on a modern firefighter's outfit and see how technology has improved.

Fascinating Facts

★ In 1666 the Great Fire started in a bakery in the appropriately named Pudding Lane, right in the centre of London. The fire destroyed most of the city and it had to be almost totally reconstructed.

★ The fire caused ten million pounds worth of damage, which is a lot even today – back then it was an enormous amount.

★ During the Great Fire of London, even the king helped to pass water buckets in an attempt to control it. Sadly his royal assistance was not enough to stop the massive inferno from spreading.

★ A famous diary writer called Samuel Pepys got caught up in the fire. Rather than worrying about his own safety, he immediately thought of how he could protect his food. He was particularly worried about his Parmesan cheese being destroyed, so he buried it in his back garden to protect it from the flames. Given the choice we'd rather save our own skin than salvage our smelly cheese!

★ The London Fire Brigade responds to over 130,000 calls each year. Only 30,000 of these are actually about fires! The rest include false alarms, road accidents, animal rescues and a whole load of other unusual emergencies. Maybe they should change their name to 'The Sticky Situation Brigade'!

Top Tip
You have to book in advance to visit the museum. Sign up for one of the fascinating twice-daily tours and an expert will take you round.

← One of London's fire engines

PLAN YOUR VISIT 34

London Fire Brigade
Winchester House, 94a Southwark Bridge Road, SE1 0EG

www.london-fire.gov.uk

📞 020 8555 1200 ext: 39894

🕐 Mon-Fri: tours at 10.30 & 14.00
Advance booking only

⊖ Borough / Southwark / Elephant & Castle

£ 🎁

I want to go here ☐

GET EXECUTED

...at the London Dungeon

Normally we wouldn't recommend being killed. But at the London Dungeon it's just so much fun. And the best thing is, you don't actually die!

The London Dungeon is a guided attraction showing gory events from London's history. Death is everywhere – there is a section on Jack the Ripper (a famous London serial killer) and another about a murderous hairdresser. Real actors wander round and jump out at you, making the whole thing even more terrifying.

Our favourite bit is the execution. You are sentenced to death by hanging, then suddenly a dramatic drop ride plunges you down into darkness. You have to be at least one metre and twenty centimetres to take part, but don't worry; if you're not tall enough there's still plenty here to fill you with fear!

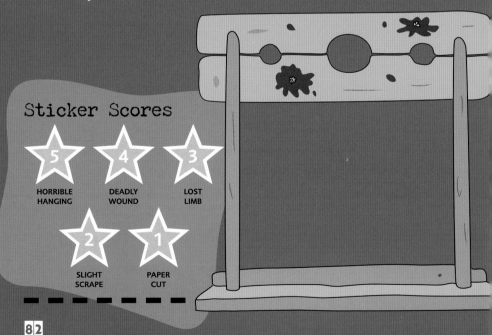

Sticker Scores

5 HORRIBLE HANGING

4 DEADLY WOUND

3 LOST LIMB

2 SLIGHT SCRAPE

1 PAPER CUT

Top Tip

The London Dungeon can be pretty scary so only go if you're prepared to be freaked out! The museum normally recommends that visitors are twelve or over – but younger kids will be allowed in.

Did you hear about the man who killed his victims by stuffing cornflakes in their mouths?

The police say they are looking for a *cereal* killer!

← He's behind you!

Fascinating Facts

★ One of London's nastiest (and smallest) dungeons is called 'Little Ease' and is hidden under the Tower of London. It measures four feet square, and was so small that any prisoner had to crouch constantly. Guy Fawkes, who tried to blow up the houses of Parliament, was put there for a day after his arrest.

★ Jack the Ripper is the name given to a real but unidentified serial killer who operated in east London in the late 1800s. The mysterious Mr Ripper would cut his victims' throats before mutilating the body. Sometimes he'd even remove peoples' vital organs.

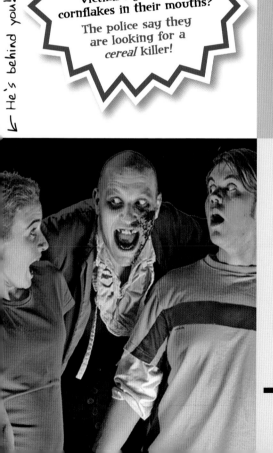

PLAN YOUR VISIT 35

The London Dungeon

28 –34 Tooley Street, SE1 2SZ
www.the-dungeons.co.uk/london

📞 **0207 403 7221**

🕐 **Opening times vary monthly, tours last 1.5 hours**

⊖ London Bridge

£££ 🎁 ❗

I want to go here ☐

LEARN ABOUT LONDON'S HISTORY

...at the Museum of London

Since London was established by the Romans, it has been hit by plagues, bombs, fires and financial disasters. Yet despite everything it has become one of the world's most important places. You just can't keep a good city down . . .

The Museum of London tells the story of the city from the first inhabitants 450,000 years ago right up to the present day. It contains over two million objects, so don't even try to see them all!

Sticker Scores

5 BEAUTIFUL BLACK CAB

4 PRETTY PHONE BOX

3 ROCKING ROUTEMASTER

2 ESSENTIAL UMBRELLA

1 RUBBISH WEATHER

We particularly like the Roman exhibits – there are lots of old coins and even a Roman bikini! And if you get tired of all that ancient history, you can go and play in the recreated 1950s living room. It's kitted out with a TV, sofa and even some traditional toys from the period.

Best of the Rest

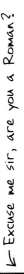

← Excuse me sir, are you a Roman?

Peer at a Penny Farthing (a Victorian bicycle) on the Victorian Walk – a reconstructed street complete with a barbershop, toy shop and chemists. With an oversized wheel at the front and a tiny one behind, it's quite unlike the modern day bike!

Choose a career using The Apprentice exhibit. You select what trade you'd like to learn, then answer a series of questions to see if you're suitable. Options include stockbroker, factory worker and seamstress.

Fascinating Facts

★ London professionals used to be famous for wearing bowler hats and carrying umbrellas. It was a sort of school uniform for bankers and businessmen.

★ In prehistoric times, elephants and lions used to live in London in the area around Trafalgar Square! Presumably they all moved out because the rent was too expensive . . .

Similar Spots

Museum of London in the Docklands has an interactive gallery where you can search for hidden treasures, play with pulleys and try on a diver's helmet.
www.museumindocklands.org.uk

PLAN YOUR VISIT 36

Museum of London
150 London Wall, EC2Y 5HN
www.museumoflondon.org.uk

📞 **020 7001 9844**

🕐 **Daily 10.00-18.00**

⊖ **Barbican / St Paul's**

FREE 🍴 🎁 ☂

I want to go here ☐

WEST LONDON

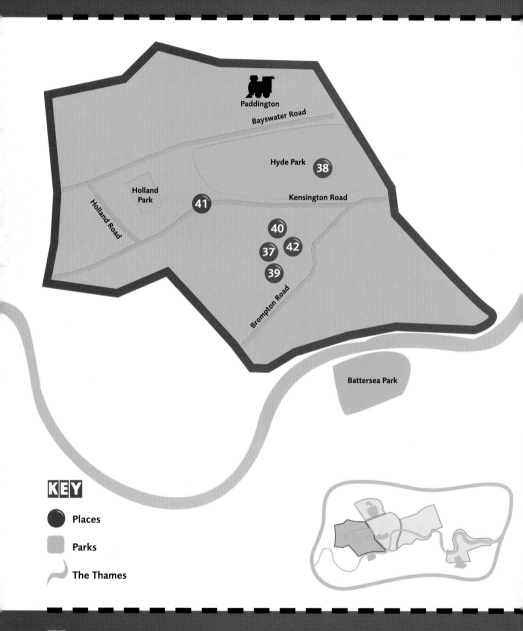

Paddington

Bayswater Road

Hyde Park

38

Holland Park

Holland Road

Kensington Road

41

40

37 42

39

Brompton Road

Battersea Park

KEY

● Places

▢ Parks

~ The Thames

CENTRAL

NORTH

SOUTH & EAST

WEST

GREENWICH

AROUND

ACROSS

TOP FIVES

STARE A T.REX IN THE EYE

...at the Natural History Museum

T he Natural History Museum's vast collection of stuffed animals, skeletons, creepy-crawlies and fossils is heaven for eco-enthusiasts. But the museum's star attraction is its terrifying tyrannosaurus rex.

Yes, we know dinosaurs have been extinct for ages. But the Natural History Museum has brought them back to life – sort of – by creating a moving model of a T.rex. Clever technology allows it to watch you as you dodge round the room. It also has a disturbing habit of roaring, before fixing you with a menacing stare, as if deciding whether you would make a tasty lunchtime snack. We dare you to stare back!

Sticker Scores

5 — TERRIFYING TYRANNOSAURUS

4 — TOUGH TRICERATOPS

3 — DECENT DIPLODOCUS

2 — MEASLY MAMMAL

1 — PATHETIC PLANT

Best of the Rest

🔑 Be wowed by a Blue Whale. The museum has a life-sized model of this colossal creature – the biggest animal that's ever lived. Its heart is the size of a small car (but less likely to get you to school on time!).

🔑 Keep an eye out for the 78 carved monkeys clambering across the ceiling of the museum. One is eating an apple.

🔑 Peer at precious stones in the vault, which contains diamonds, emeralds and even a rock from the Moon.

🔑 Walk from one end to the other of the enormous replica diplodocus skeleton.

← Who are you looking at?

Fascinating Facts

⭐ Dinosaurs became extinct approximately 65 million years ago. There are lots of theories as to what killed them – a big famine, disease, broccoli – but no one knows for sure. Most people believe a massive meteor hit the earth and caused lots of dust to fly up. This stopped the plants from growing, so there was no food and everything died.

What do you get when dinosaurs crash their cars?
Tyrannosaurus Wrecks!

WEST

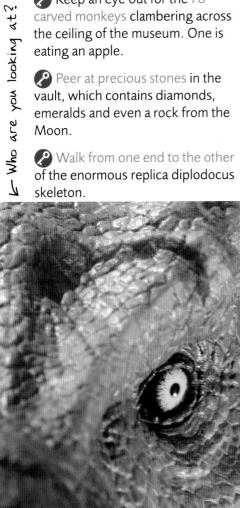

PLAN YOUR VISIT 37

Natural History Museum
Cromwell Road, SW7 5BD
www.nhm.ac.uk
📞 020 7942 5000
🕐 Daily 10.00-17.50
⊖ South Kensington
FREE 🍴 🎁 ☂

I want to go here ☐

SWIM WITH SWANS

...at Hyde Park Lido

Some indoor pools have cool stuff, like slick slides and fabulous flumes. But at this outstanding outdoor pool you can actually swim alongside swans. That's *swan* thing you won't find at your local baths!

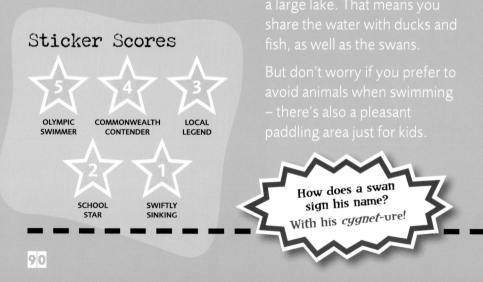

Lidos are open-air swimming pools. In the 1930s people were dead keen on swimming, so they built lidos all across London.

The Serpentine Lido is particularly special as it's a fenced-off part of a large lake. That means you share the water with ducks and fish, as well as the swans.

But don't worry if you prefer to avoid animals when swimming – there's also a pleasant paddling area just for kids.

Sticker Scores

⭐ 5 — OLYMPIC SWIMMER

⭐ 4 — COMMONWEALTH CONTENDER

⭐ 3 — LOCAL LEGEND

⭐ 2 — SCHOOL STAR

⭐ 1 — SWIFTLY SINKING

How does a swan sign his name? With his *cygnet*-ure!

Best of the Rest

🔑 Hire a rowing boat on the Serpentine.

🔑 See the park on horseback by taking a lesson with Hyde Park Stables. **www.hydeparkstables.com**

Similar Spots

🔑 Kensington Gardens lies just to the west of Hyde Park. It's home to the Princess Diana Playground, which we think is one of the best in the city. There's a gigantic pirate ship to play on, plus a jungle gym, swings, slides and roundabouts. **www.royalparks. gov.uk/Kensington-Gardens**

🔑 Holland Park is possibly London's poshest park. There's a paddock where you can see peacocks, a cricket pitch, tennis courts and a beautiful Japanese garden. There's also an adventure playground with mini climbing wall, swings, climbing frame and aerial runway. **www.rbkc.gov.uk**

← Swan Lake?

Fascinating Facts

⭐ **During the 1100s, the king decided that the royal family owned all the swans in Britain. That's still the case today.**

⭐ It's been against the law to kill swans in Britain for hundreds of years. The law says that swan-assassins can be fined or even sent to jail. Apart from the fact it's illegal, it isn't very nice for the birds.

⭐ **Swans can fly at speeds of up to 60mph. That's about the same speed as a car driving along a motorway. We presume they don't stop at any service stations along the way!**

WEST

PLAN YOUR VISIT 38

Serpentine Lido
Hyde Park, W2 2UH
www.royalparks.org.uk

📞 **0207 706 3422**

🕐 **Daily (summer) 10.00-18.00**

⊖ **Knightsbridge / Lancaster Gate**

£ ✕

I want to go here ☐

TASTE THE WORLD'S BEST CUPCAKE

...at the Hummingbird Bakery

What's the secret of a good cupcake? In our opinion it's all about loading on as much butter icing as possible. And nobody sticks on more sweet stuff than the Hummingbird Bakery.

The cupcake comes from America and is a bit like the British fairy cake. It is designed to be just big enough for one person – so don't be tricked into sharing yours! They contain butter, sugar, eggs and flour, and then you can add just about any topping you want.

Sticker Scores

5 QUADRUPLE CHOCOLATE

4 LEMON & HONEY

3 TOFFEE & WALNUT

2 BREAD & TOMATO KETCHUP

1 SPROUTS & MUD

Our favourite Hummingbird variety is the Red Velvet – a red-coloured cocoa cake with a cream-cheese topping. *Mmm!*

Fascinating Facts

★ **Cupcakes got their name because when they were invented people measured out the ingredients using cups instead of weighing scales.**

★ In 2008 the world's largest cupcake was baked – it was over one metre wide! We're also guessing that the eater of the world's largest cupcake had the world's most painful stomach-ache in 2008 . . . !

★ **The world record for cupcake eating was set in 2012, when an American man scoffed 72 in six minutes!**

WEST

↖ Eat me!

Photo Op

Take a snap of yourself scoffing a cupcake hands-free. Remove the case (with your hands) and then eat it (no hands allowed).

Note: This might embarrass your parents if you do it in the bakery, so you can use it as a good excuse to get them to buy you another cupcake to take home and practise on.

PLAN YOUR VISIT 39

Hummingbird Bakery
47 Old Brompton Road, SW7 3JP
Other venues across London
www.hummingbirdbakery.com

📞 020 7851 1795

🕐 **Mon-Thu & Sun 09.00-19.00,
Fri-Sat 09.00-20.00**

⊖ South Kensington

£ ✕ ☂

I want to go here ☐

GET IN A SPIN

...at the Science Museum

Have you got what it takes to perform the perfect spin? Well, you can find out at the Science Museum by having a go on this *revolution*-ary exhibit!

Rotation Station is one of many activities in the Science Museum's Launchpad area. Climb on board and start spinning with your bum sticking out. Then start straightening up and you'll notice how you suddenly pick up speed. This is the same technique used by ice skaters, some of whom can reach a dizzying 400 rotations per minute!

Sticker Scores

5 RIP-ROARING ROTATION

4 RAPID REVOLUTION

3 STANDARD SPIN

2 WEAK WHIRL

1 TERRIBLE TURN

Look out for other great experiments in Launchpad, including a giant wall of bubbles and a thermal imaging camera which shows you which parts of your body are the hottest.

Best of the Rest

🔑 Power a lightbulb in Pedal Power (also in Launchpad). Use the pedals and hand-cranks to generate enough electricity to power up objects including a light, a hairdryer and a TV.

Make A Day Of It

🔑 Play games and learn about global warming in the Energy Gallery.

🔑 Explore the Pattern Pod, where you can follow in the footprints of all kinds of animals.

Fascinating Facts

⭐ Ever wondered why you feel dizzy after you've stopped spinning? It's all to do with your body's balancing system. When you whirl around, fluid in your inner ear moves about and this tells your brain that you're in motion. The fluid continues to move once you've come to a stop, so your body is tricked into thinking that it's still rotating. This is what makes your head spin!

⭐ In March 2011, a man in Pakistan spun a frying pan on his finger for a record-breaking 34 minutes and 30 seconds. What a stu-*pan*-dous performance!

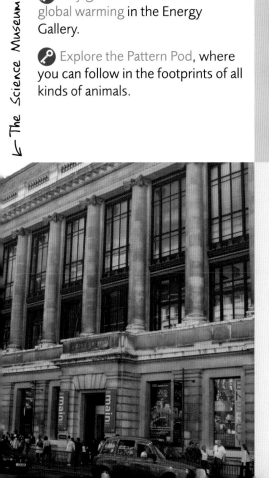

← The Science Museum

PLAN YOUR VISIT 40

The Science Museum
Exhibition Road, South Kensington, SW7 2DD
www.sciencemuseum.org.uk

📞 **0870 870 4868**

🕐 **Daily 10.00-18.00**
Closes at 19.00 during school holidays

⊖ **South Kensington**

FREE ✗ 🎁 ☂

I want to go here ☐

WALK AROUND A ROOFTOP GARDEN

...at the Roof Gardens

It's easy to make room for a garden in the countryside. But in London space is tight. So some years ago a shop in Kensington came up with a clever idea: *why not build a garden on the roof?*

Today these gardens are called The Roof Gardens and are open to the public. And we're not just talking about Astroturf and a couple of pot plants. They are the biggest roof gardens in Europe, covering one and a half acres – that's the size of a football pitch! However, you definitely won't be able to play football while you're there. These are pretty, ornamental gardens, with flamingos, ducks, trees, and even a flowing, fish-filled stream.

Sticker Scores

5 PERSONAL PARK

4 GIGANTIC GARDEN

3 VILLAGE GREEN

2 BORING BACKYARD

1 MUSTARD & CRESS

Fascinating Facts

⭐ **The gardens are home to four pink flamingos. They are called Bill, Ben, Splosh and Pecks.**

⭐ The rooftop is 30 metres above street level, which is as tall as 25 pink flamingos standing on each other's heads.

⭐ **The Hanging Gardens of Babylon in Iraq were one of the Seven Wonders of the Ancient World. Sadly they were destroyed nearly 2,000 years ago, but we think The Roof Gardens in Kensington are one of the wonders of modern London.**

> **Why does a flamingo lift up one leg?**
> Because if it lifted up both legs it would fall over!

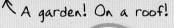

↖ A garden! On a roof!

Top Tip
The gardens are open to the public for free. However, they're sometimes booked for private parties, so you should make sure you ring ahead to check availability.

Top Tip
If you are going to the restaurant as well as the gardens, try to go on Sunday lunch time when a magician performs tricks between 12.30 and 3 p.m.

WEST

PLAN YOUR VISIT 41

The Roof Gardens in Kensington

99 Kensington High Street, W8 5SA
(access via Derry Street)

www.roofgardens.virgin.com

📞 **0207 937 7994**

🕐 **Opening hours vary – check website or call in advance**

⊖ **High Street Kensington**

FREE 🍴

I want to go here ☐

DESIGN YOUR OWN COAT OF ARMS

...at the Victoria and Albert Museum

The V&A is one of the biggest design museums in the world. Their exhibits cover everything from furniture to fashion and some go back 3,000 years.

The British Galleries also contain plenty of interactive things to do. Here you'll find a clever computer which helps you design a coat of arms. Back in the old days having a coat of arms showed that you were super-important. All noble families had one. At the Victoria and Albert museum, you can create your own and become prince or princess of the playground! You choose a colour, some pictures and the size, and the computer does the rest.

Sticker Scores

5 KING'S COAT OF ARMS

4 PRINCE'S PICTURE

3 EARL'S EMBLEM

2 SOLDIER'S SHIELD

1 COMMONER'S CREST

Best of the Rest

🔑 Borrow a backpack at the Information Desk and use it to help guide you round the galleries.

🔑 Dress up as a clown and other characters, in the Theatre & Performance Galleries. You can also use a special computer to make sound effects of wind and thunder.

🔑 See some seriously sparkly stuff in the Jewellery Gallery.

Top Tip
The children's author Jacqueline Wilson has designed her own trail which you can use to explore the museum. You can download it from the V & A website.

← The world's first museum restaurant

Fascinating Facts

★ In one of the galleries there is a giant plaster statue of a naked man called David, from the biblical story of David and Goliath. When Queen Victoria came to visit the museum the owners were worried she would be shocked by his nudity, so they added a fig leaf to the sculpture to disguise David's danglies!

★ The V&A was the first museum in the world to have a public restaurant. It has kept the original design (though fortunately not the original food) and is well worth a visit.

★ To ensure that the collections stay in top condition, 800 small radio transmitters are positioned throughout the V&A to record the temperature. They check a room's temperature and humidity every three minutes. All those old exhibits do need looking after . . .

PLAN YOUR VISIT 42

Victoria and Albert Museum
Cromwell Road, SW7 2RL
www.vam.ac.uk

📞 020 7942 2000

🕐 Sat-Thu 10.00-17.45, Fri 10.00-22.00

⊖ South Kensington

FREE ✕ 🎁 ☂

I want to go here ☐

WEST

GREENWICH

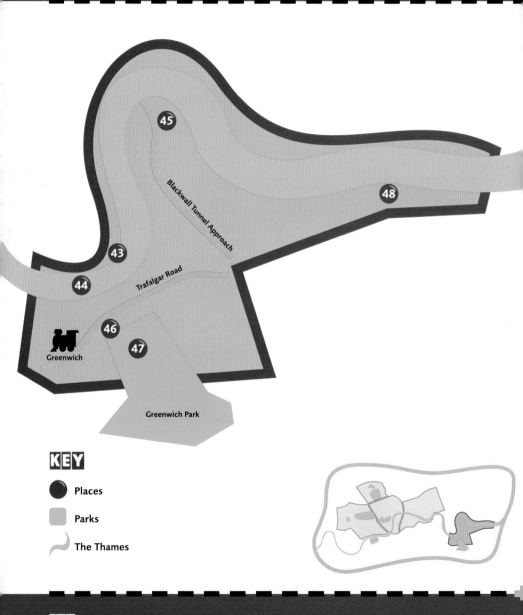

45

Blackwall Tunnel Approach

48

43

44

Trafalgar Road

46

47

Greenwich

Greenwich Park

KEY

Places

Parks

The Thames

CENTRAL

NORTH

SOUTH & EAST

WEST

GREENWICH

AROUND

ACROSS

TOP FIVES

ROUND UP THE ANIMALS

...at Mudchute City Farm

The Mudchute area was originally a dump for dug-up mud and stone when the nearby Millwall Docks were built. It might not sound glamorous, but it is perfect for a grassy, muddy city farm.

Mudchute is home to the largest city farm in London. As you'd expect it has cows, pigs and sheep, but it's also home to donkeys, llamas and all kinds of birds. In total there are over 200 animals on the farm. There's a pets' corner, where you can meet animals up close. And if you come at the beginning or end of the day you can even help staff round up the animals.

Sticker Scores

5 LEGENDARY LLAMA

4 CURIOUS COW

3 PORKY PIG

2 DOPEY DONKEY

1 EMPTY FIELD

Our favourite part is the duck walk between the farmyard and the duck pond. It's *quack*ing good fun!

Best of the Rest

🔑 Go horseriding in the riding school, which has around 25 horses and ponies. There are even showjumps and cross-country fences if you're an expert rider.

🔑 Eat fab food at the Mudchute Kitchen, where all the food is home-made by top chefs.

🔑 Play outside in Millwall Park's playground, just next to Mudchute Park.

Top Tip

The most fun way of getting to Mudchute is on the driverless DLR trains. Because they start and stop automatically, you can sit in the space at the front and pretend to be in charge!

← Duck!

Similar Spots

🔑 London's got more than ten city farms, so it's worth checking to see if there's one near you. Here are a few of the more central ones:

- Kentish Town City Farm (north)
- Spitalfields City Farm (east)
- Hackney City Farm (east)
- Vauxhall City Farm (south)
- Deen City Farm and Riding School (south west)

PLAN YOUR VISIT 43

Mudchute Park and Farm
Pier Street, Mudchute, E14 3HP
www.mudchute.org

📞 020 7515 5901

🕐 Daily 08.00-16.00

⊖ Mudchute (DLR)

FREE 🍴 🎁

I want to go here ☐

WALK UNDERNEATH THE THAMES

...through the Greenwich Foot Tunnel

Walking on water is generally not possible for people without superhuman powers. But anyone can walk *under* water by taking a stroll through the Greenwich Foot Tunnel.

The Greenwich Foot Tunnel is a pedestrian crossing beneath the Thames – from Greenwich to the Isle of Dogs. You enter through the pretty, round brick houses at either end. Ignore the creaky old lifts and take the stairs instead – count the steps as you go down.

In the tunnel, if you listen carefully, you can hear water swooshing overhead. It can be quite spooky – sometimes there are even drops of water falling from the ceiling.

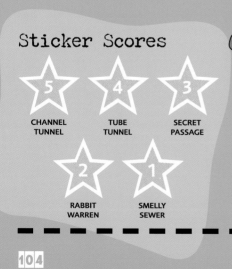

Sticker Scores

5	4	3
CHANNEL TUNNEL	TUBE TUNNEL	SECRET PASSAGE

2	1
RABBIT WARREN	SMELLY SEWER

Inside the Greenwich Foot Tunnel

Fascinating Facts

⭐ **The foot tunnel was opened in 1902, to allow dock workers who lived to the south of the Thames to get to their jobs on the Isle of Dogs. Before then they had to take a ferry, which was expensive and unreliable.**

⭐ Nowadays the workers using the tunnel are mostly people travelling from their homes (on the south side) to their office jobs in Canary Wharf (on the north side). So don't try walking south through the tunnel at 08.00 or north at 18.00, as you'll be going in the opposite direction to everyone else!

⭐ **The tunnel is over 370 metres long. A tunnel this long would take the average mole around 67 hours of continual work to dig. Although the mole's tunnel would be less likely to include white tiles and strip lights!**

GREENWICH

Photo Op
Stand in the middle of the tunnel and make a star shape with your body. Try to get the photo when no one else is visible behind you.

 **PLAN YOUR VISIT** 44

Greenwich Foot Tunnel
Access via Cutty Sark Gardens (in Greenwich) or Island Gardens (on the Isle of Dogs)

🕑 **Open 24 hours**

⊖ **Greenwich (DLR and rail)**

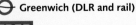 FREE

I want to go here ☐

FLY THROUGH THE SKY

...on The Emirates Airline

Public transport can be a bit boring, but you won't be yawning on the Emirates Airline. Trust us, the time will fly by!

The Emirates Airline is a cable car linking the north and south sides of the river Thames. It opened in June 2012, just in time to be an important transport route for London's Olympic Games.

The cabins are glass-fronted, so on a clear day you'll get great views of the city below you. Look out for amazing aerial views of the O2 Arena and Canary Wharf. It can wobble a bit when it's windy, but don't worry, the cable keeps it stable!

Sticker Scores

5	4	3
FIRST CLASS	FLIGHT OF FANCY	PLANE SAILING

2	1
FLY FISHING	HOT AIR

Best of the Rest

 Catch a movie at the multIplex cinema in the 02 Arena, which has the UK's largest 3D screen. The 02 is the giant dome-shaped building next to the Greenwich Peninsula terminal on the south side of the river. It hosts concerts and shows throughout the year. **www.theo2.co.uk**

← Don't leave me hanging!

Top Tip
You can use an Oyster card on the Emirates Airline, just like on the rest of London's transport network. Make sure yours is topped up before you arrive to avoid queuing for tickets.

Fascinating Facts

★ **The cabins 'fly' along a cable, which is held up by three steel towers. They reach a maximum altitude of 90 metres, which is roughly the same height as Big Ben!**

★ The Emirates Airline route linked two important Olympic venues during London 2012. The O2 Arena on the south side hosted basketball and gymnastics, while the ExCel centre on the north side was home to seven sports including weightlifting and table tennis.

★ **The highest cable car system in the world is in Mérida, Venezuela. It reaches up to 4,765 metres high above sea level. Sounds fairly fr-*height*-ening to us!**

GREENWICH

PLAN YOUR VISIT 45
The Emirates Airline
Greenwich Peninsula (south terminal), Unit 1, Edmund Halley Way, SE10 0FR
www.emiratesairline.co.uk

🕐 **Mon-Fri 07.00-20.00**
Sat 08.00-20.00
Sun 09.00-20.00

⊖ North Greenwich

£

I want to go here ☐

STEER A VIRTUAL SHIP

...at the National Maritime Museum

Obviously the best place to sail a ship would be on the sea. But for that you need years of training, whereas the Maritime Museum's ship simulator is open to everyone.

The National Maritime Museum is about everything to do with ships and the sea. The ship simulator is similar to the real machines used to train ship captains. You can choose to take control of a rescue ship on its way towards a sinking vessel, or navigate through New York harbour. It's impressively realistic – you feel the vibrating engine and hear the screeching seagulls. You're scored on how well you do, so why not challenge a family member to a sailing showdown? It's *sea*-riously good fun.

Sticker Scores

⭐ 5 WARSHIP

⭐ 4 CRUISE LINER

⭐ 3 RACING YACHT

⭐ 2 DINKY DINGHY

⭐ 1 RUBBER DUCKY

Best of the Rest

Load a cargo ship in the interactive Children's Gallery. You can also prepare food in the ship's galley and even fire a cannon!

Similar Spots

Walk the decks of a world-famous ship. The Cutty Sark is a nineteenth-century-tea clipper – a fast sailing ship that carried tea and other precious cargo around the world. The ship was badly damaged by fire in 2007, but has now been restored to its former glory. **www.rmg.co.uk**

Anchors outside the National Maritime Museum

NATIONAL MARITIME MUSEUM

GREENWICH

One ship carrying blue paint collided with another ship carrying red paint. The sailors are believed to be marooned!

Photo Op
Strike a naval pose while standing at the controls of the ship simulator. Put your hand on your head in a salute, and adopt a serious expression as you look out across the (imaginary) waves. *Aye-aye, Captain!*

PLAN YOUR VISIT **46**

National Maritime Museum
Greenwich, SE10 9NF
www.rmg.co.uk

📞 **020 8858 4422**

🕐 **Daily 10.00-17.00**

⊖ **Greenwich (DLR and rail)**

FREE 🍴 🎁 ☂

I want to go here ☐

109

LOOK INTO A CAMERA OBSCURA

...at the Greenwich Royal Observatory

What is a camera obscura? Well, it's actually Latin for darkened room. And, strangely enough, that's exactly what it is!

Before modern cameras were invented, people discovered that if you made a small hole in the side of a dark building, a clear picture of what was going on outside appeared inside the room. And it moved in real time, like a television screen.

At the Greenwich Royal Observatory, the camera obscura projects the outside world onto a large circular table. It works best in bright weather, when you can spy on unsuspecting passers-by. Try and catch someone scratching their bum or picking their nose!

Sticker Scores

5 MOVIE MULTIPLEX

4 IMAX CINEMA

3 WIDESCREEN TELLY

2 PANORAMIC PAINTING

1 SLOPPY SCRIBBLE

Best of the Rest

🔑 Touch some ancient rock and see how stars and planets are born, in the Astronomy Galleries. The rock is almost four billion years old – nearly as old as the Earth itself. Imagine how many candles you'd need on that birthday cake!

🔑 Visit London's only planetarium – the Peter Harrison Planetarium. You can watch a show about space and the planets, and see one of the world's most modern digital laser projectors.

🔑 Gaze at a giant telescope. It's one of the largest of its type in the UK and is over 100 years old. It sits in the building's curious onion-shaped roof.

Fascinating Facts

⭐ The observatory is also the site of the Greenwich Meridian – the line which divides the earth into its east and west hemispheres. All distances and times on Earth are measured in relation to this point. At night a laser beam shines out from the observatory. This is partly to show where the meridian is, and partly just to amaze ya with a really big laser!

Photo Op

Take a picture of yourself standing in two different halves of the world, with one foot either side of the Greenwich Meridian.

PLAN YOUR VISIT 47

Royal Observatory
Blackheath Avenue, Greenwich, SE10 8XJ
www.nmm.ac.uk

📞 020 8858 4422

🕐 Daily (summer) 10.00-18.00
Daily (out of season) 10.00-17.00

🚇 Greenwich (DLR and rail)

£ 🍽 🎁 ☂

I want to go here ☐

← The Peter Harrison Planetarium

SEE LONDON'S FLOOD DEFENCES

...at the Thames Barrier

The Thames Barrier protects the city from high tides and flooding (which saves millions of people from getting wet feet!).

The barrier is a massive construction on the Thames near Woolwich. It was first used in 1983, and stretches all the way across the river. (It wouldn't work very well if it didn't!)

It's best seen from the river, and several of London's boat services go out to the barrier. There is a good information centre there, but not all boats stop, so plan your route in advance if you want to visit.

Sticker Scores

5
RAGING
RIVER

4
TREMENDOUS
TORRENT

3
SPARKLING
STREAM

2
BUBBLING
BROOK

1
DISMAL
DRIBBLE

Best of the Rest

Let off some steam at the playground in Thames Barrier Park, on the north side of the river. There's also a fountain display to splash around in.

What's worse than when it's raining cats and dogs?
Hailing taxis!

The Thames Barrier →

Fascinating Facts

★ **The Thames Barrier is the second largest movable flood barrier in the world. It's a whopping 520 metres long, which is more than double the length of Tower Bridge.**

★ When raised, the barrier's main gates are as tall as a five-storey building. They weigh 3,300 tonnes, which means each gate is as heavy as 165,000 reef sharks.

★ **Rising tides caused by climate change have caused some experts to worry that the barrier will struggle to cope with water levels as early as 2015. So make sure you own a good pair of wellies!**

GREENWICH

AROUND LONDON

Luton

Stanstead

51

49

50

City

60
54

Heathrow

58

52

59

61

53

57

56

55

Gatwick

KEY

● Places

▬ Parks

〰 The Thames

CENTRAL

NORTH

SOUTH & EAST

WEST

GREENWICH

AROUND

ACROSS

TOP FIVES

FLY A FIGHTER JET

...at the Royal Air Force Museum

OK, so it's not a real fighter jet, but the flight simulator at the Royal Air Force (RAF) Museum is as realistic as you'll get without years of training.

The RAF Museum is in a giant aircraft hangar, so there's plenty of space for the exhibits. It contains 100 full-sized aircraft from around the world, including machines from the very early years of flight as well as the latest modern jets. There are also two simulators in the museum.

You can be part of the Red Arrows, take a trip in a Tornado (a combat aircraft) and even experience a dogfight (that's the name for a battle between aeroplanes – no real dogs are harmed!).

Sticker Scores

★5	★4	★3
FIGHTER JET	JUMBO JET	PROPELLER PLANE

★2	★1
GLIDER	PAPER PLANE

Best of the Rest

🔑 Climb into a cockpit and touch part of a real aircraft in The Aeronauts Interactive Centre. You'll learn all about flight and flying, and there are fact sheets to help you find your way around.

🔑 Soar through the sky in a daring mission over enemy territory, at the 4D theatre (extra charge applies). Cutting edge animation and special effects make you feel like you really are in the cockpit.

🔑 See a sound and light show about the Battle of Britain, which the RAF fought against German aircraft during World War Two. The show takes place above real Hurricane and Spitfire aircraft, which helps recreate the atmosphere of wartime aerial combat.

Where would you like us to fly you?

Top Tip
You have to be at least one metre tall to be allowed on the flight simulators so get your tape measure out before you go. Don't worry if you're not tall enough – there are still plenty of fun things to do.

Photo Op
Get a snap of you sitting in the cockpit of a real fighter plane.

PLAN YOUR VISIT 49

Royal Air Force Museum London
Grahame Park Way, Colindale, NW9 5LL
www.rafmuseum.org.uk

📞 **020 8205 2266**

🕐 **Daily 10.00-18.00**

⊖ **Colindale**

FREE (entry) **£** (to use simulator)

I want to go here ☐

AROUND

STROLL AROUND A CEMETERY

...at Abney Park Victorian Garden Cemetery

Abney Park Cemetery is a beautiful place for a walk. Its higgledy-piggledy layout is ideal for peace and quiet. Oh, and being a cemetery, it also happens to be full of dead people . . .

Between 1800 and 1850 London's population more than doubled, and finding places to put dead bodies was a real problem. Private cemeteries (including Abney Park) sprung up, and the prettiest ones became known as the Magnificent Seven.

Over time the cemetery has developed a mysterious, haunted atmosphere, making it perfect for hide-and-seek! But if hiding amongst tombstones doesn't sound like your thing, check out the park's lovely Children's Garden which holds workshops and storytelling sessions.

Sticker Scores

5 — CRACKING CEMETERY

4 — BRILLIANT BURIAL GROUND

3 — GRAND GRAVEYARD

2 — MODERATE MEMORIAL

1 — BARE BONES

R.I.P. V.I.P.

Similar Spots

All the Magnificent Seven are great for a stroll, and are (mostly) free of charge. Three of our favourites are:

Highgate Cemetery (north).
Use their leaflet to find gravestones of dead famous people, including philosopher Karl Marx. There is an entrance charge.
www.highgate-cemetery.org

Nunhead Cemetery (south).
One of the least known but prettiest of the Magnificent Seven, the cemetery is full of sad stone angels and beautiful monuments.
www.southwark.gov.uk

Brompton Cemetery (west).
Over 35,000 monuments sit among wildlife such as birds, foxes and squirrels in this quiet resting place. Brompton has also featured in the films *Goldeneye* and *Stormbreaker*.
www.royalparks.org.uk

← A lion lyin' on a grave

Why do graveyards have a big wall around them?
Because everyone is *dying* to get in!

Fascinating Facts

★ From the beginning Abney Cemetery was designed for people of all religions. The ground has never been declared holy.

★ Over 200,000 people have been buried in its grounds, including the founder of the Salvation Army, William Booth.

★ In London burial space is getting so tight that local authorities are allowed to reclaim a grave that's not been used for 75 years, and take up any spare space in it!

Photo Op
Find the graceful stone lion in Abney Cemetery and then snap yourself stroking its smooth paw.

PLAN YOUR VISIT 50
Abney Park Cemetery
Stoke Newington, N16 0LN
www.hackney.gov.uk/cp-abneypark

📞 020 7275 7557

🕐 Daily (summer) 09.00-17.30
Daily (out of season) 09.00-15.30

🚃 Stoke Newington

FREE

I want to go here ☐

AROUND

HANG OUT AT HOGWARTS

...on the Warner Bros Studio Tour

You don't have to travel from platform 9 and 3/4 to get to Hogwarts . . . just take the shuttle bus from Watford Junction station!

The Warner Bros. Studio Tour is a *magical* new attraction that lets you go behind the scenes of the sets from the Harry Potter movies. You get to peer into the potions classroom, hang out in Hagrid's hut and wander round the Weasleys' kitchen.

One of the highlights is the Great Hall. Follow in the footsteps of Ron and Harry, and look out for the graffiti that's been carved into the tables by cheeky students. Then pop into Dumbledore's office for a sneaky peek at the spellbinding sorting hat. It's never been so cool to *potter* around a school!

Sticker Scores

5 MASTERFUL MAGICIAN

4 WISE WIZARD

3 COOL CONJURER

2 SAD SORCERER

1 BROKEN SPELL

Best Of The Rest

Discover the magic of green screen. This is the technological *wizardry* that was used to film amazing scenes like the quidditch matches. You can also admire Harry's Nimbus 2000 broomstick!

Similar Spots

Hogwarts' Great Hall was modelled on the hall at Christ Church College in Oxford, and several scenes from the films were shot in the college's grounds.
www.chch.ox.ac.uk

Alnwick Castle in Northumberland was used to film the exterior shots of Hogwarts in the first two films.
www.alnwickcastle.com

Goathland station on the North Yorkshire Moors railway appears on film as Hogsmeade Station.
www.nymr.co.uk

← The great hall at Hogwarts

Fascinating Facts

⭐ **The actors playing Harry and Ron outgrew their beds in the Gryffindor boys' dormitory over the course of filming the first Harry Potter movie. Some unique camera angles had to be used to hide the fact that they were now teenagers! You'll see the original beds from the film on your tour.**

⭐ The Harry Potter books have been translated into more than 67 different languages and sold a *Ron*-believable 400 million copies!

Top Tip
Tours must be booked in advance, so phone ahead or go online to secure your place.

PLAN YOUR VISIT 51
Warner Bros. Studio Tour London
Aerodrome Way, Leavesden, WD25 7LS
www.wbstudiotour.co.uk

📞 08450 840 900
🕐 **Tours start at 10.00**

£££ 🎁 ☔

AROUND

I want to go here ☐

GO BIRD-WATCHING

...at London Wetland Centre

People think of London as a bustling city, packed with buildings and busy people. So it's a surprise to find that there's a pretty, peaceful nature reserve in London on the banks of the river Thames.

The London Wetland Centre in Barnes is a lakeside area that's home to rare birds and other wildlife. Spread over 105 acres (or almost 70 football pitches), the centre contains many species that can't be found anywhere else in London.

Sticker Scores

5 WONDERFUL WATER VOLE

4 PRETTY PARAKEET

3 SWIMMING SWAN

2 DAWDLING DUCK

1 BIRD POO

It has six hides where you can watch birds without them seeing you. Head to the three-storey Peacock Hide and see if you can spot swans, ducks, parakeets, sparrowhawks, kingfishers, water voles and bats. You'd be *batty* not to.

Best of the Rest

Watch the otters being fed, twice daily at 11.00 and 14.00. The centre has a family of Asian short-clawed otters, and you can watch them swimming, playing and feasting on fish. W-*otter* treat!

Zoom down a zip wire, conquer the climbing wall and scurry through giant water vole tunnels at the outdoor playground in the Explore Adventure Zone.

Go pond-dipping in a guided session at the Pond Zone. You can also operate an underwater camera to see what's wriggling and squirming beneath the surface.

Have a splashing good time playing water games at the indoor Discovery Centre.

Is it a bird? Is it a plane?

Fascinating Facts

★ **Many species of birds live in different parts of the world at different times of year. They move to find better food, or nicer weather. These journeys are known as migration. It's a bit like the bird version of heading to Spain for the summer to top up your tan.**

★ Arctic Terns migrate from the Arctic to the Antarctic and back again every year and they sometimes drop in at the Wetland Centre on the way. During their lifetime these birds travel a distance equal to going to the moon and back. It's one small step for a bird . . . one giant leap for birdkind!

Photo Op
Get a picture of you standing underneath the giant dragonfly – he's perched on the roof of the pagoda in the main courtyard. Be warned: he buzzes if you get too close!

PLAN YOUR VISIT 52

WWT London Wetland Centre
Queen Elizabeth's Walk, Barnes, SW13 9WT
www.wwt.org.uk

📞 020 8409 4400

🕐 Daily (summer) 09.30-18.00
Daily (out of season) 09.30-17.00

Ⓤ Hammersmith

££ ✕ 🎁

I want to go here ☐

AROUND

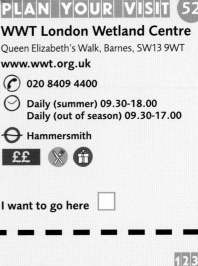

TAKE A TENNIS TOUR OF WIMBLEDON

...at Wimbledon Lawn Tennis Museum

In 1875 Major Walter Clopton Wingfield invented a new sport called *Sphairistike*. The game was popular, but the name was ridiculous, so it was renamed tennis and people have been playing it ever since.

Wimbledon is the oldest and most important tennis tournament in the world. It was first held on a grass surface in 1877 at Major Clopton Wingfield's croquet club. The Wimbledon Championships are still played there in the summer, but you can visit at any time of year.

The official tour takes in Centre Court, the press interview room and the on-site museum. There's even a 200 degree cinema which shows footage of a match from all angles. So . . . *anyone for tennis?*

Sticker Scores

5 GAME, SET AND MATCH

4 FORTY LOVE

3 THIRTY FIFTEEN

2 LOVE ALL

1 LOVE NOBODY

Fascinating Facts

★ American player Andy Roddick holds the record for the fastest serve. In 2004 he managed to biff a ball at 155 miles per hour. That's more than twice as fast as the motorway speed limit in the UK!

★ Tennis was invented to be played on grass, which is why the organisation responsible for the game in the UK is called the Lawn Tennis Association. But these days Wimbledon is the only major tournament to be played on the green stuff. The others all take place on clay or hard court surfaces.

★ When Wimbledon started it was just for men. However, a tournament for women was added in 1881.

★ The first Ladies' Singles title was won by Maud Watson, who played against her older sister Lilian. They both wore white corsets and petticoats, starting a trend for nattily dressed tennis-playing sisters.

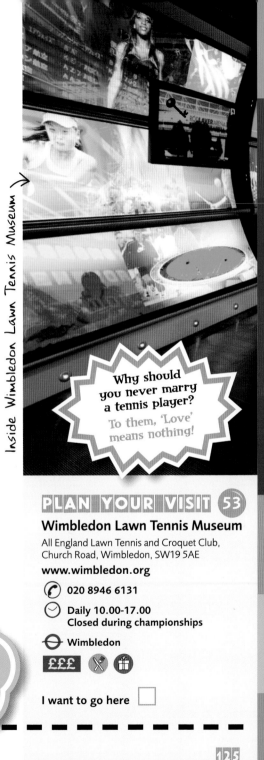

Inside Wimbledon Lawn Tennis Museum

Why should you never marry a tennis player?
To them, 'Love' means nothing!

Top Tip

Unless you have tickets for the tournament, make sure you don't plan to visit Wimbledon when the championships are taking place. They start in late June every year and last for two weeks. There are no tours during that period, and the museum is only open to spectators.

PLAN YOUR VISIT 53

Wimbledon Lawn Tennis Museum

All England Lawn Tennis and Croquet Club, Church Road, Wimbledon, SW19 5AE

www.wimbledon.org

☎ **020 8946 6131**

🕐 **Daily 10.00-17.00**
Closed during championships

⊖ **Wimbledon**

£££ 🍴 🎁

I want to go here ☐

AROUND

VISIT THE QUEEN'S FAVOURITE CASTLE

...at Windsor Castle

The royal family own *lots* of castles. People disagree on exactly how many they have, but we're pretty sure it's more than we've got. And Windsor Castle is one of the Queen's favourites.

Windsor Castle is the biggest and oldest lived-in castle anywhere in the world. The first bits were built just after 1066, when William the Conqueror was king, making it over 900 years old.

The castle is full of fascinating ancient things. Look out for the collection of armour which was once used by kings, knights and princes.

Sticker Scores

5	4	3
COLOSSAL CASTLE	PRETTY PALACE	HUGE HOUSE

2	1
COMFY COTTAGE	CARDBOARD BOX

There are even some very small suits of armour for kids! Or, if fighting's not your thing, they also have one of the most magnificent dolls' houses in the world.

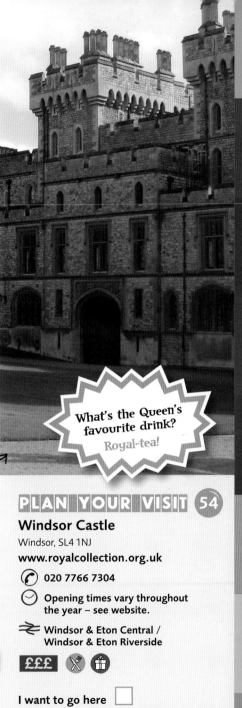

Fascinating Facts

⭐ **The castle covers 44,965 square metres. That means you could stick seven football pitches inside it and still have space for a playroom and paddling pool.**

⭐ The castle's chapel contains the tombs of ten former kings and queens, including Henry VIII.

⭐ **During one of the outbreaks of bubonic plague Queen Elizabeth I escaped to Windsor Castle. She gave orders that all visitors from London should be hanged. Thankfully this is no longer our government's formal position on how to deal with a medical crisis!**

⭐ The length of a modern marathon – 26.22 miles – is actually the distance from Windsor Castle to the old Olympic Stadium in London. This is because the 1908 London Olympians ran along this course. The race was particularly popular and this soon became the global standard.

A castle fit for a queen

Top Tip

Time your visit to see the Changing of the Guard - a colourful ceremony in which the soldiers guarding the Queen swap over. Check the website before you visit for the latest information on dates and times.

What's the Queen's favourite drink?
Royal-tea!

PLAN YOUR VISIT 54

Windsor Castle
Windsor, SL4 1NJ
www.royalcollection.org.uk

📞 **020 7766 7304**

🕐 **Opening times vary throughout the year – see website.**

🚄 **Windsor & Eton Central / Windsor & Eton Riverside**

£££ ✕ 🎁

I want to go here ☐

AROUND

RIDE A ROLLER-COASTER

...at Chessington World of Adventures

Everyone loves a roller-coaster, and this awesome adventure park is one of the best places to take the plunge.

Chessington World of Adventures is a theme park, an aquarium and a zoo all rolled into one. You can ride ripping roller-coasters in all kinds of themed lands (though some have height restrictions – see the website for more information). Alternatively check out sharks and stingrays in the Sea Life Centre or come face to face with tigers, lions and gorillas in the Trail of the Kings.

Look out for the Wild Asia attraction, where you'll find the Kobra, a spinning disk ride that is shaped like a snake. Hold on tight or you'll be *hiss*-tory!

Sticker Scores

5 ROCKING ROLLER-COASTER

4 LUSCIOUS LOG FLUME

3 WHEELING WALTZER

2 HELTER SKELTER

1 DEPRESSED DONKEY

Fascinating Facts

★ In the days before amusement parks, London had fairs to amuse the masses. The oldest is Bartholomew Fair, which ran from 1133 to 1855. It started as an event for buying and selling cloth, then developed to feature fighters, freak shows, animals and acrobats!

★ In 2007, a man from the USA broke the world record for the longest ride on a roller-coaster. He rode on the Big One at Blackpool Pleasure Beach for a staggering seventeen days!

Getting close to a meerkat at Chessington Zoo

Top Tip

Plan your trip to arrive as soon as the park opens and head straight to the biggest and newest rides, or to the furthest bits of the park first.

Top Tip

The restaurants get busier and the rides get quieter between 12.00 and 13.30. So if you have lunch either very early or very late you'll spend more time on the rides and less time in the queues.

What does a dentist do on a roller coaster?
He *braces* himself!

PLAN YOUR VISIT 55

Chessington World of Adventures
Leatherhead Road, Chessington, KT9 2NE
www.chessington.com

✆ 0871 282 5124

🕐 Daily (peak) 10.00-18.00
Opening times vary out of season

🚆 Chessington South

£££ ✗ 🎁 ❗

I want to go here ☐

AROUND

EXPLORE UNDERGROUND CAVES

...at Chislehurst Caves

Chislehurst's chalk caves were first dug around 8,000 years ago, during the Neolithic age. This is the period when people moved from hunting and gathering to farming. Supermarkets were not yet an option . . .

There are over twenty miles of mysterious, man-made chalk caves at Chislehurst. Originally they were used to mine chalky substances like lime and flint. Lime was an ingredient for primitive plaster and paint, and flint was good for making tools.

These days, you can tour the spooky caves and find out what they've been used for over the years. For example, during World War Two they made a great bomb shelter.
So even if Chislehurst is attacked during your visit, you'll probably be OK.

Sticker Scores

⭐ 5 COLOSSAL CAVERN

⭐ 4 GROOVY GROTTO

⭐ 3 COMMON CAVE

⭐ 2 PUNY POTHOLE

⭐ 1 NASTY NOOK

Fascinating Facts

★ **Chislehurst Caves are owned by a company called Kent Mushrooms, who bought them to grow mushrooms in.**

★ The largest cave in the world is the Sarawak Chamber in Malaysia. It covers an area the size of three football pitches. The roof is 70 metres high, which is the same height as 50 cavemen standing on each other's heads (though not half as hairy!).

★ **The world's longest cave is Mammoth Cave in Kentucky, USA. Over 367 miles of passages have been found and mapped there. That's longer than the distance from London to Edinburgh.**

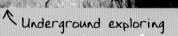

↖ Underground exploring

What did one bat say to another?
Let's *hang around together!*

Photo Op
Crouch in a cave and hold your lantern out in front of you to light the way. You will look like a true explorer!

PLAN YOUR VISIT 56

Chislehurst Caves
Old Hill, Chislehurst, Kent, BR7 5NL
www.chislehurstcaves.co.uk

📞 **020 8467 3264**

🕐 **Wed-Sun 10.00-16.00**

🚃 **Chislehurst**

£ ✗ 🎁 ☂

I want to go here ☐

GET LOST IN AN ENORMOUS MAZE

...at Hampton Court Palace

Normally, getting lost is not to be recommended. But when you visit Hampton Court's world-famous maze, it's part of the fun.
Just make sure you find your way out in time for dinner.

Hampton Court is the site of a grand old royal palace. It was built in 1514 for Cardinal Wolsey, who was a friend of Henry VIII (until Henry arrested him, anyway!). The maze was built about 175 years later, in 1690, and has barely changed since.
Split your family into teams

and race to reach the middle. Always stick with an adult – getting lost with a grown-up can be fun, but being stuck in a maze alone is not a great way to spend a day.

Sticker Scores

5	**4**	**3**
A-MAZE-ING MAZE	LEGENDARY LABYRINTH	PLEASING PUZZLE

2	**1**
RESPECTABLE RIDDLE	LOST CAUSE

Photo Op
Have your photo taken at the centre of the maze, with your arms raised in a triumphant pose.

Fascinating Facts

⭐ The world's largest maze is the Pineapple Garden Maze in Oahu, Hawaii. It has a total path length of two and half miles and is made up of 14,000 colourful Hawaiian plants, including the pineapple. As far as we know, no one has ever tried eating their way out!

⭐ Studies have shown that laboratory rats find their way out of mazes more quickly if they hear classical music playing. We're not sure if Mozart will help you get out of the maze at Hampton Court, but we reckon it's worth a try!

Top Tip

During the summer you can get to Hampton Court by boat from Westminster. The boat service also stops at places like Kew and Richmond along the way.

Best of the Rest

🔑 Watch a falconry display. This is just one of the special events that take place at Hampton Court throughout the year. You can also catch Tudor cooking festivals, old etiquette lessons and even jousting classes!

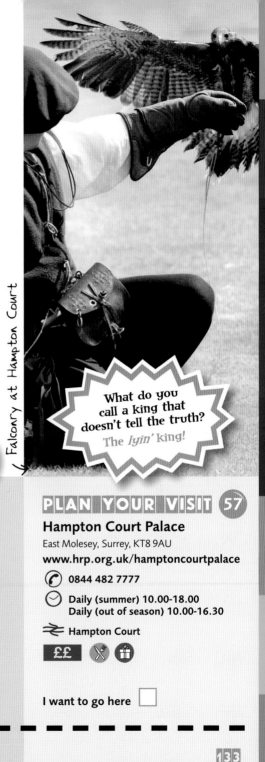

Falconry at Hampton Court

What do you call a king that doesn't tell the truth?
The *lyin'* king!

PLAN YOUR VISIT 57

Hampton Court Palace

East Molesey, Surrey, KT8 9AU

www.hrp.org.uk/hamptoncourtpalace

📞 0844 482 7777

🕐 **Daily (summer) 10.00-18.00**
Daily (out of season) 10.00-16.30

🚆 Hampton Court

££ ✗ 🎁

I want to go here ☐

AROUND

TAKE A TREE-TOP TRAIL

...at the Royal Botanic Gardens, Kew

Kew Gardens has thousands of trees, but from the ground you can only really see their trunks. So the best way to look at them in all their glory is to travel along the tree-top walkway.

Kew is home to the world's biggest collection of living plants. There are over 30,000 species in total, and 650 people are employed to look after them.

The tree-top walkway is the most exciting way to look round the gardens. It's eighteen metres off the ground (as tall as eighteen of you standing on each other's shoulders – just easier to walk along!).

Sticker Scores

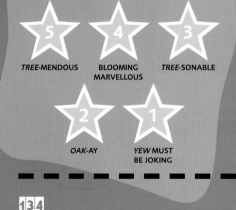

5 — *TREE*-MENDOUS

4 — BLOOMING MARVELLOUS

3 — *TREE*-SONABLE

2 — *OAK*-AY

1 — *YEW* MUST BE JOKING

After taking the stairs up to the walkway, snake through the trees while admiring the view. *Tree*-mendous!

Best of the Rest

🔑 Clamber across rope bridges and whizz along a zip wire in the Treehouse Towers play area.

🔑 Check out the enormous compost heap. As well as being as being an environmentally friendly dump for Kew's garden waste, it's also where poo from the army's horses is deposited.

🔑 Peer at a piranha in the Princess of Wales Conservatory.

← Travelling through the tree-tops

Top Tip

You can picnic anywhere apart from inside the cafes and restaurants, and there are plenty of spots to scoff your sandwiches in scenic surroundings.

Fascinating Facts

⭐ **Trees are the oldest living things on Earth. The oldest ones discovered are a cluster of spruce trees in Sweden, which are around 8,000 years old and still going strong.**

⭐ The world's largest flower is the *Titan Arum*. It can grow up to three metres tall – the size of a small tree. It's also one of the smelliest plants, and it has the scent of rotting meat. This pong attracts insects that would normally feed on dead animals. That's a bit like wearing a poo-perfume to impress someone you fancy!

What's black, highly dangerous and lives in a tree?

A crow with a machine gun!

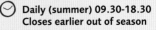
PLAN YOUR VISIT 58

Royal Botanic Gardens
Kew, Richmond, TW9 3AB
www.kew.org

📞 020 8332 5655

🕐 **Daily (summer) 09.30-18.30**
Closes earlier out of season

⊖ Kew Gardens

FREE 🍴 🎁

I want to go here ☐

AROUND

SCRUM DOWN

...at Twickenham

Like many ball sports, rugby is a game of skill, with lots of passing and kicking. Unlike most sports however, it is played with a funny-shaped ball and you are allowed to run into each other!

Twickenham Stadium (or Twickers, as it's known to fans) has been the home of English rugby since 1910, when it held a crowd of 20,000 people. Nowadays it takes four times as many rugby fans.

You can visit Twickenham stadium and museum at any time of year. The stadium tour takes you into the players' dressing room (hopefully they'll have picked up their sweaty socks) and beside the pitch. Then head over to the museum to test your strength on their scrum machine.

Sticker Scores

5 TRY!

4 PENALTY

3 CONVERSION

2 SCRUM DOWN

1 TRY HARDER . . .

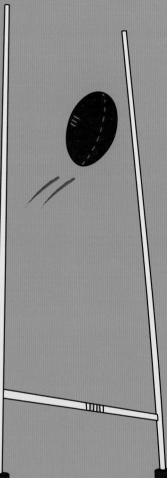

Fascinating Facts

⭐ Rugby developed during the 1800s from a form of football played at Rugby School in Warwickshire. The boys there used an oval ball made from an inflated pig's bladder. In 1823 a pupil called William Webb Ellis started running with the ball in his hands. At the time this was considered cheating, but a brand-new game was created from his way of playing. So, the next time you're playing a game and get told off for a foul, just tell the referee you're inventing a new sport!

⭐ Streakers are spectators who for some foolish reason chose to run naked onto the pitch. The first ever example of this at a major sporting event was at Twickenham in 1974. A man called Michael O Brien stripped off and ran out during a game. He was captured by a policeman who cleverly covered Michael's dangly bits with his police helmet.

⭐ There are several forms of rugby played around the world today. Rugby union is the full name for the sort played at Twickenham. Another version is rugby league, which is particularly popular in the north of England. The other well-known form in the UK is rugby sevens, where teams have, unsurprisingly, seven players.

Running out on to the pitch

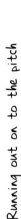

PLAN YOUR VISIT 59

Twickenham Stadium
Rugby Road, Twickenham, TW1 1DZ
www.rfu.com/microsites/museum

📞 020 8892 8877

🕐 Tue-Sat 10.30-15.00, Sun 13.00-15.00

🚆 Twickenham

£££ ✗ 🎁

I want to go here ☐

AROUND

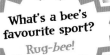

What's a bee's favourite sport?
Rug-*bee*!

WALK THROUGH A LEGO LONDON

...at Legoland Windsor

Not all names describe a place accurately. For example, Greenland is covered in ice and Iceland actually has quite a few green bits. Thankfully Legoland is exactly what you'd expect – it's a theme park made of Lego!

Legoland has everything other theme parks have – rides, slides and attractions. The difference is that in Legoland anything that can be made of Lego *is* made of Lego. There are Lego buildings, Lego Vikings and even Lego cars you can drive.

The most impressive Lego creation is Miniland. This area contains buildings from London and other cities all created entirely from Lego. Look out for Lego landmarks like Big Ben, the London Eye and Tower Bridge (and to read about the real things go to pages 20, 34 and 60).

TELEPHONE

Sticker Scores

5 LEGO LONDON

4 LEGO CAR

3 LEGO PYRAMID

2 LEGO VIKING

1 *LEGO* OF MY LEG

Best of the Rest

🔑 Learn to drive at the Legoland Driving school. You are given an electric car and get to drive it round a course that includes traffic lights and roundabouts.

🔑 Be a pirate for the day at the Pirate Training Camp. You can learn some seafaring and swashbuckling skills, before testing your nerve (and your stomach) on the swinging pirate ship.

Photo Op
Find your favourite mini-building and pose next to it for a snap.

← Miniland looks like this, but made of Lego!

Fascinating Facts

⭐ **Lego was invented in Denmark. The name comes from the Danish words leg godt, which mean 'play well'.**

⭐ If all the Lego bricks ever made were divided up between every living person, we'd all end up with 62 each.

Top Tip
There are sometimes large queues at Legoland, but you can avoid standing in line for each attraction by using the clever Q-Bot system. Details are on the website.

PLAN YOUR VISIT 60

Legoland Windsor
Winkfield Road, Windsor, SL4 4AY
www.legoland.co.uk

📞 0871 2222 001

🕐 Daily 10.00-18.00
Varies out of season

🚆 Windsor & Eton Central

£££ ✕ 🎁

I want to go here ☐

AROUND

PLAY WEIRD MUSICAL INSTRUMENTS

...at the Horniman Museum

There was more to Frederick Horniman than a silly name. He was an English politician, tea trader and collector who founded a fascinating museum filled with anything and everything.

The Horniman Museum contains so much it's hard to describe. The museum says that it promotes understanding of the world, environments, peoples and cultures. We say it's got loads of cool stuff and you need to see it to appreciate it!

The Music Gallery in the museum has twelve thousand weird and wonderful instruments on display. You can even play some of them yourself. Why not try the dulcimer – a sort of cross between a xylophone and a banjo. We think it's *strum*-thing special!

Sticker Scores

5 — OUTSTANDING ORCHESTRA

4 — BRASS BAND

3 — JAZZ QUARTET

2 — ONE-MAN BAND

1 — ELASTIC BAND

Best of the Rest

🔑 Admire aquatic creatures from Moon jellyfish to seahorses at the museum's aquarium.

🔑 Play giant musical instruments in the outdoor Sound Garden. The museum has 16 acres of beautiful gardens, so there's plenty of room to run about.

Top Tip
The Horniman puts on great events, so check online before you go to see what's happening. You may be able to catch a concert, or listen to a storyteller.

Fascinating Facts

⭐ **The oldest instrument in the museum is a pair of bone clappers shaped like human hands. They come from Egypt and were probably made around 1,500 B.C.**

⭐ Outside the museum there is a twenty-metre-tall totem pole. It was carved in 1985 by Nathan Jackson, an American Indian from Alaska. His clan crest, the eagle, sits at the top of the pole.

Photo Op
Pick your favourite musical instrument and pose while you play it in the music gallery.

← Listening to music in the music gallery

PLAN YOUR VISIT **61**

Horniman Museum and Gardens
100 London Rd, SE23 3PQ
www.horniman.ac.uk

📞 **020 8699 1872**

🕐 **Daily 10.30–17.30**

🚃 **Forest Hill**

FREE 🍴 🎁 ☂

AROUND

I want to go here ☐

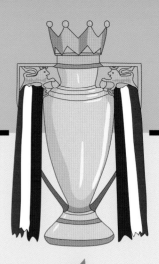

CENTRAL
NORTH
SOUTH & EAST
WEST
GREENWICH
AROUND
ACROSS
TOP FIVES

TAKE A TUBE

If you've never been on a tube train before, you're in for a treat. The tube is basically a network of trains rushing through tunnels below London under the ground. That's right. UNDER. THE. GROUND. What's not to love?

Each tube tunnel is known as a line and has stops at regular points along the way. The first tube line opened in 1863 with open carriages running on coal power. All that fuel being burned made it stinky and smoky, so in 1890 they started to use electricity to run the trains instead. All tube lines are fun the first time you use them, though the Jubilee's our favourite. It's the newest, and some of the stations have a funky, futuristic design.

Sticker Scores

5 THE TUBE
4 YOU TUBE
3 TUBA
2
1

Comedy Drivers

🔑 Occasionally, tube drivers make funny announcements. Here are some of our favourites from the past few years.

"Ladies and gentlemen, upon departing the train may I remind you to take your rubbish with you. Despite the fact that you are in something that is metal, fairly round, filthy and smells, this is a tube train and not a bin on wheels."

"Next time, you might find it easier to wait until the doors are open before trying to get on the train. The big slidey things are the doors, you can see by the way they open and shut."

"Apparently, this train is no longer terminating at Barking, it's terminating here. I'm sorry about this but I also thought it was going to Barking. I mean, why tell me – I'm just the driver . . ."

← Mind the gap!

Fascinating Facts

★ **The tube is one of the busiest travel systems in the world. It carries over four million passengers per day. That's more than the entire population of Wales.**

★ You'll sometimes see pigeons catching the underground. The clever birds travel a couple of stops on the tube to save their wings, particularly when carriages are empty.

★ **Angel station (part of the Northern line) has the longest escalator in Europe. In 2006 someone actually skied down it (and posted the video on YouTube). We really do not advise you to try this yourself.**

★ During World War Two, the tube was used as a shelter. People ate, slept and even gave birth in it.

PLAN YOUR VISIT 62

www.tfl.gov.uk

£

I want to do this ☐

FLOAT ON A BOAT

Today the Thames is clean enough for fish to live in it, but this hasn't always been the case. In 1858, the river contained so much sewage that the pong caused parliament to be abandoned. It became known as 'the smelly summer'.

The river Thames flows through the centre of London. It has always been an important part of the city as a route for carrying cargo and people.

During the 1600s and 1700s the Thames froze every winter. People skated along the river, and there were even fairs and bonfires on top of it. These days you can't skate on the Thames, but you can take a boat along it. There are several companies that run tourist trips, but it's often easier to take the Transport for London passenger ferries, which stop off at various interesting points along the way.

Sticker Scores

⭐ 5 — **BOTTLED WATER**

⭐ 4 — **TAP WATER**

⭐ 3 — **SEA WATER**

⭐ 2 — **PUDDLE WATER**

⭐ 1 — **WAT-ER DISGRACE**

Best of the Rest

In addition to the well-known stuff, there are plenty of other things to look out for on your river cruise. Here are some of our favourites:

Cleopatra's Needle, near Embankment pier, is a 3,500 year old stone obelisk from Egypt.

Battersea Power Station looks a bit like a huge, upside-down snooker table. It's been inactive since 1982, but is now finally being redeveloped to house hundreds of luxury riverside flats.

The **Oxo Tower**, opposite the Embankment, was bought in 1920 by the people who make Oxo stock cubes. They were refused permission to put up a neon sign with their name on it, so they cheekily made windows in the shape of O X O instead!

Blackfriars Bridge is the place on the Thames where the tide turns. Look out for carvings of freshwater birds on west side and sea birds on the east side.

Ferry good fun!

Why was the Thames angry?

Because it had been *crossed* so many times!

PLAN YOUR VISIT 63

Timetables & prices vary
www.tfl.gov.uk
www.citycruises.com
www.flyingfishtours.co.uk

£ – £££

I want to do this ☐

ACROSS

147

HOP ON A ROUTEMASTER

No trip to London is complete without riding on a big red bus. And if you pick the right route, you can even take a trip on one of the classic Routemaster models.

London has a massive choice of bus routes, so you can use them to get just about anywhere. On most routes the traditional double-decker bus – known as the Routemaster – has been replaced by more modern designs. However it does still run every fifteen minutes on two special heritage routes. The number nine (which runs between the Royal Albert Hall and Aldwych) and the number fifteen (which runs between Trafalgar Square and Tower Hill) both feature Routemasters from 09.30 to 18.30.

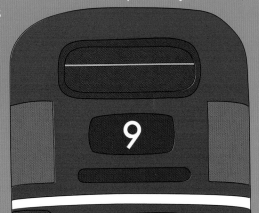

Sticker Scores

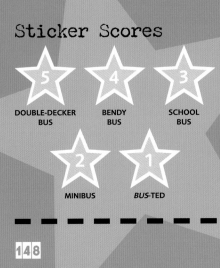

5	4	3
DOUBLE-DECKER BUS	BENDY BUS	SCHOOL BUS

2	1
MINIBUS	*BUS*-TED

A row of Routemasters

Fascinating Facts

⭐ **There are over 17,500 bus stops in London. 12,000 of these have shelters to protect customers from the rain. The other 5,500 are not great places to be in a storm.**

⭐ More buses have been added to London's streets in the past decade. This means fewer people need to use cars, which is better for the environment. In 2006 there were more than 1.8 billion bus journeys around the capital.

⭐ **The first London bus arrived in 1829, when a horse-drawn carriage ran from Paddington to Bank. London finally got motorised buses in 1908, and the horses got a holiday.**

PLAN YOUR VISIT 64

www.tfl.gov.uk

Photo Op
Get a snap of you at the front of the top deck of a Routemaster bus. It's absolutely the best place to sit.

I want to do this ☐

ACROSS

RIDE A DUCK

Like real ducks, DUKWs are amphibious, which means they can move in water and on land. Unlike ducks, though, they can't quack.

During World War Two, DUKWs were very useful as they reduced the time required to load stuff on and off ships. They would ferry cargo so that big navy ships didn't have to come into a port. Today they're used for taking tourists round London.

The DUKW route goes past Big Ben and Trafalgar Square before leaving the road behind and floating down the Thames. It's the most fun you'll ever have sitting on a duck.

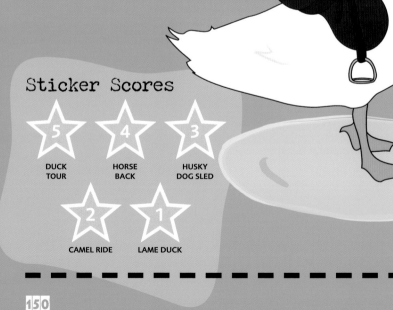

Sticker Scores

5 DUCK TOUR	4 HORSE BACK	3 HUSKY DOG SLED
2 CAMEL RIDE	1 LAME DUCK	

Fascinating Facts

⭐ **DUKWS were first used in the D-Day landings (a very important part of World War Two which began on 6 June 1944). Over 21,000 DUKWS were used that day to take Allied (British, American and Canadian) troops ashore.**

⭐ Although the DUKWS were very useful during World War Two, their importance decreased once helicopters were invented.

⭐ **DUKWS were originally used by the military, but police, fire stations and other rescue units soon caught on. There was even a group of fishermen who bought one to take their catch directly into market.**

↖ Like a duck to water

What happens to ducks who fly upside down?

They *quack up!*

Top Tip
If you're planning to take a duck tour during the summer, make sure you buy your tickets in advance online. The tours are very popular, and can get booked up a week or more ahead.

PLAN YOUR VISIT 65

London Duck Tours
55 York Road, SE1 7NJ
www.londonducktours.co.uk

📞 020 7928 3132

I want to do this ☐

RUN THROUGH THE PLAYERS' TUNNEL

...at Wembley Stadium

Wembley has been the home of English football since 1923. So if you plan on becoming a sporting superstar, there's no better place to get a taste of your future fame.

Wembley is not only a venue for major football matches. It also plays host to rugby league, American football and even the occasional pop concert.

On the Wembley tour you'll get to see the players' dressing rooms, the television interview room and the trophy winners' steps. There's also marvellous memorabilia, including the crossbar from England's 1966 World Cup win. But we reckon the best bit is running through the tunnel towards the pitch. Just think – the next time you visit, you might be taking part in a big game . . .

Sticker Scores

5 WORLD CUP

4 PREMIER LEAGUE

3 CHAMPIONSHIP

2 SUNDAY LEAGUE

1 MUCK UP

Why was Cinderella rubbish in goal?
Because she ran away from the ball!

Similar Spots

🔑 The Emirates Stadium is Arsenal's home ground. The club offers terrific tours – you can even upgrade to the Legends Tour and be guided around by an ex Arsenal star! **www.arsenal.com**

🔑 Chelsea play at Stamford Bridge in south-west London. Check the website for details of their access-all-area tours. You can even arrange a private one, just for your family and friends. **www.chelseafc.com**

Top Tip
Tours don't run on match days, so check in advance to see what's available.

← Wembley's impressive arch

Fascinating Facts

⭐ **Wembley's striking arch can be seen right across London. It's 133 metres tall, which is the about same height as 12,000 chocolate bars stacked on top of each other (though less likely to melt in the sun).**

⭐ The Jules Rimet Trophy (a replica of which you can see on the Wembley Tour) has had an eventful history. In March 1966, it was stolen from the museum where it was on display. A dog named Pickles sniffed it out a week later, and when England won the cup in July that year Pickles was invited to the celebration banquet to lick the plates clean!

PLAN YOUR VISIT 66

Wembley National Stadium
Wembley, HA9 0WS
www.wembleystadium.com

📞 0844 800 2755
🕐 Daily 10.00-18.00 (call to confirm)
🚆 Wembley Stadium
⊖ Wembley Park

£££ ✕ 🎁 ☂

I want to do this ☐

ACROSS

HOP OVER TO PARIS

We know Paris is not actually in London, but you can get there and back in a day on the Eurostar train. It's by far the most expensive thing in this book, and a trip there is a terrific treat.

Paris is the capital of France. It's also a place of good food, beautiful buildings and grumpy people talking French. The Eurostar is a super-speedy train that connects Paris with London. It goes under water, through the Channel Tunnel between Dover and Calais. You depart from St Pancras station, and within two and a half hours you're in the centre of Paris!

There's so much to do there that we'll never cover it all on these two pages. So who knows, maybe we'll write a whole book about the place!

Sticker Scores

5 HIGH-SPEED TRAIN

4 FAST CAR

3 TRUNDLING TRAM

2 CHUGGING COACH

1 WEARY WALKING

Best of the Rest

🔑 Get an eyeful of the Eiffel Tower, and take the lifts to the top of this world-famous structure. Then go and play in one of the three playgrounds in the nearby Champs de Mars Park.

🔑 Gaze at gargoyles in Notre Dame Cathedral, and climb the cathedral's South Tower for a stunning view of Paris. Then go to the Berthillon ice-cream shop on the Île Saint-Louis.

🔑 Climb to the top of the Arc de Triomphe and look out across Paris. Then walk down the Champs-Elysées and do some shopping on the way. If you're feeling really energetic you may even get all the way to the Louvre museum. This is the home of the Mona Lisa – the world's most famous painting.

What do you call a French Flea?
A Paris-ite!

Photo Op
Buy a baguette (a French loaf of bread) and strike a pose next to the Eiffel Tower.

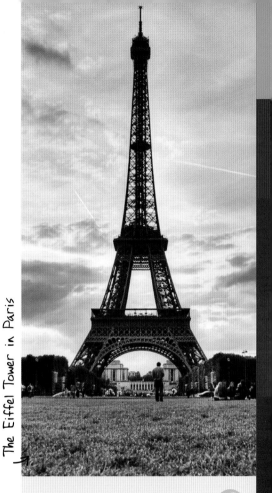

The Eiffel Tower in Paris

PLAN YOUR VISIT 67

Paris, France
Umm, not in London at all actually
www.eurostar.com

📞 0870 5186 186

£££££

I want to do this ☐

CENTRAL

NORTH

SOUTH & EAST

WEST

GREENWICH

AROUND

ACROSS

TOP FIVES

TOP FIVE

...things to spot in London

While you are out and about on the streets of London, be sure to keep an eye out for these unique things.

I SPOTTED:

- [ ] Taxi Shelter
- [ ] Drinking Fountain
- [ ] Dragon
- [ ] Blue Plaque
- [ ] Street Art

Taxi Shelters

Drinking Fountains

They might look like garden sheds, but these green boxes are actually shelters for cabbies (slang for London taxi drivers).

61 were built between 1874 and 1914 to provide somewhere other than the pub for cabbies to hang out. The shelters provided decent food and hot drinks at reasonable prices. Thirteen still exist around London – you can find good examples at Hanover Square, Russell Square and Warwick Avenue.

Hanover Square Taxi Shelter

Hanover Square Westminster, W1S

It used to be impossible to get a free drink of water in London. So in 1859 a politician called Samuel Gurney set up a fund to pay for public drinking fountains.

As well as facilities for humans, cattle troughs were installed for thirsty horses and dogs. Fountains and troughs can still be found all over London. The first one is in the wall of St Sepulchre's Church on Holborn Viaduct.

St Sepulchre's Church Drinking Fountain

St Sepulchre's Church, Holborn Viaduct, EC1A 2WY

Dragons guarding the City of London

Blue Plaques

Street Art

For hundreds of years the main entrances to the City of London have been guarded by dragons.

Good ones to look out for include the metal dragon on a pillar in Fleet Street and the four ancient, weather-beaten dragons which support the Monument. However, there are plenty of others in nooks and crannies around the city. As well as the statues, you'll see dragon carvings engraved on bridges, walls and even rubbish bins!

Fleet Street Dragon

Outside Royal Courts of Justice, Fleet Street, EC4

In 1867, the Royal Society of Arts started putting up plaques around London to acknowledge the homes or working places of famous dead people.

The first one was put up for the poet Lord Byron. There are now around 300 blue plaques in London, with about twelve more added each year. To get one you need to either be 100 years old, or have been dead for twenty years.

Samuel Morse Blue Plaque

Cleveland Street, W1

Street art – or graffiti – involves spray-painting pictures on walls and buildings. It's illegal, but the best stuff is sometimes tolerated by London's authorities.

The most famous graffiti in London is by a mysterious artist known as Banksy. Over his career he has caught the eye of famous fans including Brad Pitt and Christina Aguilera. His works are all over London – two particularly popular spots are Shoreditch and Waterloo.

Yellow Lines Flower Painter by Banksy

Pollard Street, E2

TOP FIVE

...places to shop for toys and sweets

London's got some of the best toy and sweet shops in the world. Don't forget, many museums have great toy shops attached too. The Museum of Childhood (p54) and the British Museum (p10) are two of the best.

Hamleys
(central)

Harrods
(central)

Hamleys has been a toy shop for over 250 years. Fortunately, the toys it sells are newer than the building.

The store sells magic scientific toys, remote-control airplanes, kites, board games, Lego and pretty much everything else you could ever want. You don't even need to buy anything to have fun – you can just wander round watching the toy demonstrations and magic shows.

Hamleys
188-196 Regent Street, W1B 5BT
www.hamleys.com

Harrods is the biggest department store in London.

On sale are some of the most expensive toys on the planet, including a £10,000 car for kids! Fortunately there are also cheaper things to buy. Go to the Animal Kingdom and see pampered pets, or *hoof* it to the tack shop where you'll find a huge selection of horse accessories. And don't miss the candy shop, where you'll find a big chocolate fountain.

Harrods
87-135 Brompton Road, Knightsbridge, SW1X 7XL
www.harrods.com

The Disney Store (central)

Cybercandy (central)

Greenwich Market (central)

Are you a mate of Mickey Mouse, or a fan of Hannah Montana? If so, the Disney Store is the place to go.

You'll find toys, clothes and DVDs based on these and other Disney characters. There are several Disney Stores in London, so check the website to see if there's one near you. Or, if you want the biggest and best store, head to the main House of the Mouse on Oxford Street.

This shop's got a massive range of sweets and drinks from around the world.

You can sample sugary stuff from countries including America, Japan, Australia, New Zealand, South Africa, Canada, Finland, Sweden and Mexico. And, of course, they also stock the best of British sweets. Why not buy one of the mystery parcels of sweets, or pick 'n' mix your own selection? *Sweet!*

Greenwich Market has two tremendous traditional shops for games and sweets:

Compendia sells traditional games and jigsaws – you won't find anything here that needs a plug or batteries.

Mr Humbug is a traditional sweet shop – the shelves are stacked with big glass sweet jars alongside traditional slabs of home-made toffee and fudge. Best of all, the prices are old-fashioned too!

The Disney Store
360–366 Oxford Street, Mayfair, W1C 1JN
www.disneystore.co.uk

Cybercandy
3 Garrick Street, Covent Garden, WC2E 9BF
www.cybercandy.co.uk

Greenwich Market
Greenwich
www.compendia.co.uk
www.mrhumbug.com

TOP FIVE

...markets

London's markets contain an amazing mix of junk and treasure. You never know what will turn up for sale. In the past we have found antique books, weapons, cheap kettles, gold swords, toys, stuffed crocodiles, ancient stamps and a spoon. These markets are five of our favourites, but it's worth checking out which markets are near you. They're almost all worth a visit!

I WENT TO:

- ☐ Brick Lane Market
- ☐ Portobello Market
- ☐ Camden Lock Market
- ☐ Borough Market
- ☐ Columbia Road Flower Market

Brick Lane Market (east)

Portobello Market (west)

Brick Lane Market is a place where all kinds of cultures collide.

Indian sari shops jostle with second-hand clothes stores. Jewish bagel shops squash up next to Bangladeshi curry houses. In short, you can get most things you want here, and a lot you don't. For example, there used to be a stall that only sold rusty cog wheels. It's a true East End London experience.

Brick Lane Market

Brick Lane, E1
Sun 08.00-14.00

There's been a market on Portobello Road since 1870, and it's now the longest in London.

It has different sections, moving from antiques to fruit and veg to fashion and second-hand stuff. Model sharks, old football kit and ornamental daggers have all been spotted here (not in the vegetable section, obviously). Street performers compete with shouty vegetable sellers to see who can make the most noise.

Portobello Market

Notting Hill, W11
Opening hours vary

Camden Lock Market (north)

Borough Market (south)

Columbia Road Flower Market (east)

Often overcrowded, the six markets at Camden are nevertheless a brilliant place to see some seriously strange stuff (and some even stranger people).

It's a bit like a mini-festival, with music blaring, people performing and fabulous fancy dress. The Middle Yard is surrounded by stalls selling every type of food. The water bus from Little Venice and London Zoo stops at the nearby canal lock (p42), so you can arrive in style.

Camden Lock Market

Camden Lock, NW1
Open all week, but busiest on Sundays

Borough Market is the London food-lover's favourite place.

It's full of tasty things from all around the world and home to some very specialist businesses. There's a stall that just sells one type of cheese, and another selling hundreds of types of bread. Most stallholders let you try things for free, so make sure you don't eat before you go! Whatever you try, we reckon you'll find it Borough-ly delicious.

Borough Market

Southwark, SE1
Thu-Sat (opening hours vary)

This flower market is *bloomin'* marvellous!

When you arrive you are hit by an explosion of colours and smells. The streets behind the main stalls are also home to some interesting small shops. You'll find bread, cheese, antiques, candlesticks and Buddhist artefacts all on sale. The market used to be home to a notorious gang who murdered orphans and sold their bodies. We prefer the modern use!

Columbia Road Flower Market

Columbia Road, Shoreditch, E2 7RG
Sun 08.00-14.00

TOP FIVE

...places to run around

London has hundreds of parks, from tiny squares to massive heaths. Here are five of the best. We've also included some information on parks elsewhere in this book – check out Hyde Park on p90 and Regent's Park on p40.

I WENT TO:

- [ ] Battersea Park
- [ ] Hampstead Heath
- [ ] Coram's Fields
- [ ] Richmond Park
- [ ] Crystal Palace Park

Battersea Park (south)

Hampstead Heath (north)

Battersea Park is stuffed full of fun things to do. Its zoo is a particularly popular spot.

You can pet goats, pat ponies, or just watch the monkeys scrambling around. Elsewhere in the park you'll find an adventure playground, sub-tropical gardens and a fountain lake. In the summer months you can also go boating on the park's pond or rent a three-wheeled bike.

Battersea Park
Battersea, SW11 4NJ
www.batterseapark.org

This is the wildest of the London parks, with a hilly mix of grass and woodland.

Its attractions include three outdoor swimming pools, a playground and a pond for model boats. Kenwood House, to the north of the Heath, is also well worth a visit. It is home to all kinds of events throughout the year like bat-spotting, fireworks, classical concerts and a famous Easter-egg hunt.

Hampstead Heath
Highgate Road, Camden, NW3 7
www.hampsteadheath.net

Coram's Fields (central)

Richmond Park (around)

Crystal Palace Park (around)

Coram's Fields is a park just for kids – adults are only allowed in if they bring a child.

Inside you'll find a paddling pool, slides, swings and even a small farm with sheep, rabbits and goats. The park used to be the site of a home for abandoned children, established by Thomas Coram in 1739. Now you don't have to be abandoned to use the park's facilities; you just need to be under sixteen.

Coram's Fields
95 Guilford St, Bloomsbury, WC1N 1DN
www.coramsfields.org

Richmond is London's largest park. It's also the only one to be home to over 600 deer.

You can ride through it on horseback by hiring a horse from the nearby stables. Or you can opt for two wheels instead of four legs and hire a bike. The park has places to fish, watch wildlife and eat. You can also check out one of the two playgrounds at the Kingston Gate and Petersham Gate entrances.

Richmond Park
Surrey, TW10 5HS
www.royalparks.org.uk

This park is the unlikely site of the world's first dinosaur sculptures, which are around 150 years old.

Unlike dinosaurs, which have been extinct for 65 million years, the original sculptures still survive. Whilst they're no longer considered very scientifically accurate, they're still pretty impressive. The park also has a playground, a sports centre and a farm containing all kinds of animals (but no dinosaurs).

Crystal Palace Park
Crystal Palace, SE19
www.crystalpalacepark.org

TOP FIVE

...party ideas

London's a great place to hold a party. Here are five of our favourite ways to have fun with your friends. Of course, many of the places in this guide book would also make great party venues. So you need never be short of ideas for a big birthday bash!

I WENT TO:

- ☐ Gambado
- ☐ The Castle Climbing Centre
- ☐ Sharky and George
- ☐ Coral Reef
- ☐ All Star Lanes

Hang out in a children's play centre

Gambado centres are really brilliant places to have a party.

They are designed especially for kids and they have lots of stuff to play on as well as all kinds of different activities. There's a giant playframe, laser games, climbing walls, slides, obstacle courses . . . just too many things to list them all here! We particularly like the dizzifying dodgems, and the charming carousel is also good fun.

Gambado

Various locations – check website for details
www.gambado.com

Go climbing in a castle

If you've ever got into trouble for climbing where you shouldn't, this place is heaven.

The Castle Climbing Centre is in an old converted pumping station and looks just like a castle. It's full of places to climb safely with an instructor's supervision. Parties are organised by the Geckos Climbing Club, which operates at the centre and puts on all kinds of courses and events for kids. Age restrictions apply.

The Castle Climbing Centre

Green Lanes, Stoke Newington, N4 2
www.castle-climbing.co.u

Have a Sharky and George party

Party in a pool

Go bowling

Sharky and George are a company dedicated to running brilliant parties for you in the comfort of your own home.

Sharky holds the record for running 100 metres while dressed as a pantomime horse. George drives a London taxi. These are people you would want organising your birthday. As well as their classic party, you can also choose to have your day themed around things such as cooking, movies or sports.

Sharky and George
They come to you!
www.sharkyandgeorge.com

Fancy hosting a party that will really make a *splash*? Then Coral Reef, just west of London, is the place for you.

As well as the swimming pool, there are water slides, fast flowing rapids, and even a pirate ship which you can swim around! They have special birthday party packages where everyone gets a meal, an activity pack and a pirate hat. Get ready, get set, get wet!

Coral Reef
9 Mile Ride, Bracknell, RG12 7JQ
www.bracknell-forest.gov. uk/coralreef

Bowling is a giggle wherever you go, but our favourite venue is the All Star Lanes at Whiteleys Shopping Centre.

It has a 1950s American theme, which makes it a very stylish place to hold a party. You can either bowl in the main area or hire a private room that looks like a hunting lodge from the Wild West. There's also a great party menu, with munchies, milkshakes and cakes. *Strike!*

All Star Lanes
Whiteleys, 6 Porchester Gardens, W2 4DB (Other branches in Holborn and Brick Lane)
www.allstarlanes.co.uk

TOP FIVES

TOP FIVE

...places to watch a film

Not all cinemas are the same! Many London cinemas have clubs for kids, or special features like swanky seats. Here are five interesting and unusual places to see a groovy movie.

I WENT TO:

- [ ] **IMAX**
- [ ] **Leicester Square**
- [ ] **Everyman Cinema**
- [ ] **Electric**
- [ ] **Ritzy Cinema**

IMAX (south)

The IMAX is the biggest cinema screen in the UK.

At around 20 metres high and 26 metres wide, it covers the same amount of space as 1,000 widescreen televisions. It shows a mixture of popular movies and 3D films made specifically for the IMAX screen. You watch the films through a special pair of glasses, to get a thrilling 3D effect.

IMAX
1 Charlie Chaplin Walk, Southbank, SE1 8XR
www.bfi.org.uk

Leicester Square (central)

There are five big cinemas to choose from in London's Leiceste Square, which is the location for most of the film premieres in the UK.

Busy, buzzing, and constantl full of people, there are a whole load of bright lights and entertainment options. Cheap it's not, but this is the heart of London, and if you'r lucky, you might even get to see the stars walking down the red carpet.

Odeon Leicester Square Odeon Mezzanine, Emp Odeon West End, Vue
Leicester Square

Everyman Cinema (north)

Electric (west)

Ritzy Cinema (south)

These cinemas are pretty expensive, but that's because the seats are comfy sofas and velvet armchairs!

And the luxury is not limited to the seating – the Everyman also stocks fabulous food and drink. So you can sit back and watch the film while tucking into a brownie or chomping on cheesecake. The Belsize Park branch has special screenings just for kids on Saturday mornings.

Everyman Cinema

5 Holly Bush Vale, Hampstead, NW3 6TX

203 Haverstock Hill, Belsize Park, NW3 4QG

www.everymancinema.com

The Electric is another posh cinema. This one is on Portobello Road in Notting Hill, and has swanky leather seats.

There are special Kids Club screenings on Saturday mornings, showing all your favourite films. Why not combine your visit with a stroll through Portobello market (p162) If you're a big film buff you might also want to sign up for one of the regular film workshops.

Electric Cinema

191 Portobello Road, W11 2ED

www.electriccinema.co.uk

The Ritzy Cinema is one of London's few remaining traditional cinemas.

It's based in a grand old building in Brixton and opened in 1911. Like the Electric, the Ritzy runs a Saturday morning Kids' Club, showing a selection of films for children up to fifteen years old. If you become a member of the club, you are even offered the chance to start the film on your birthday!

Ritzy Cinema

Brixton Oval, Coldharbour Lane, SW2 1JG

www.picturehouses.co.uk

PARENTS' PAGE

Hello. This page isn't for children to read. It's only for adults. So if you're a child stop reading now. We said stop. As in stop reading. STOP. Now. If we were you we'd go straight to page 78 and find out how you can sleep on a pirate ship. Still reading? OK, fine. Carry on if you really want to. But it's going to be less interesting than the rest of the book. Don't say we didn't warn you.

So anyway, hello, adult.

London Unlocked is for children who are visiting places with adults. Very few of our sites admit unaccompanied children. So as you're likely to be the one planning the trip, we've included site details such as telephone numbers and opening hours on each page. Bear in mind that most sites are closed for Christmas, and that last admission is usually earlier than the closing time. We've also specified if there are height or age restrictions. While we have tried hard to ensure all the details are accurate at the time of going to press, things change, so it's best to check before you go anywhere.

Next, a quick word about the Internet. We've tried to make sure that all our weblinks are child-friendly, but all the same, we suggest you supervise any surfing. We take no responsibility for third-party content and we recommend you check a site first if you are at all unsure.

Now for some general tips:

- Quite a few venues run good workshops and activities during weekends and school holidays. These are sometimes free, but may require advance booking.

- Many of the activities can be combined into a single day out. Use the maps at the beginning of each section to work out what things are near each other.

- Some of the activities in our book could be dangerous without appropriate adult supervision. Children using this book should be accompanied at all times.

Because we don't want you to feel left out, here are some facts about London that we've selected just for you. They're more boring than the facts in the rest of the book, obviously. But you're an adult, so you won't mind that.

- London's first Lord Mayor was Henry Fitz-Ailwyn, a draper who took office in 1189. You may remember him from your childhood.
- Today London has both a Lord Mayor of the City of London and a Mayor of London. They are part of a bipartite administration, consisting of the strategic city-wide part (the Greater London Authority) and a local part containing 33 district authorities. The GLA is run by the Mayor, who has executive powers, and the London Assembly (also elected). The Lord Mayor is head of the City of London Corporation, one of the 33 district authorities.
- Are you seriously still awake? Gosh, you really do have an appetite for boring details, don't you? Fair enough, we'll press on . . .
- Central London is a big city for business. Over half of all FTSE 100 companies have their headquarters here. Yawn . . .
- London was first named *Londinium* by the Romans. Twelfth-century cleric Geoffrey of Monmouth wrote an influential book giving details on life in Roman London entitled *Historia Regum Britanniae*. Find a copy and read it if you must.
- Franz Joseph Haydn, the Austrian classical composer, wrote twelve works dedicated to London. They are known as the 'London Symphonies' and were written between 1791 and 1795. We've never heard them but apparently adults like them.
- The Royal Albert Hall has more than 13,500 letter As engraved in the banisters and stonework throughout the building.
- There are over seven million people living in London at a population density of 12,331 per square mile. The wider metropolitan area is estimated to contain some thirteen million individuals.
- Using the Koppen climate classification, London can be said to have a temperate marine climate. This means that the city rarely sees extremely high or low temperatures. Summers have average daytime high temperatures of 22 °C (70 °F), whereas winters have average daytime highs of around 10 °C (46 °F). But frankly, this information is completely useless to you because the weather in London is never average.
- London is an anagram of noodln.

Right, we think that's everything. So now please give the book back to your kid. Or, if you're a child and you've waded through all this, now move on to a more interesting page. Seriously, move along. There's nothing more to see here.

INDEX

...here's an index of all the places included

CENTRAL
NORTH
SOUTH & EAST
WEST
GREENWICH
AROUND
ACROSS
TOP FIVES

INDEX

Where can you . . .

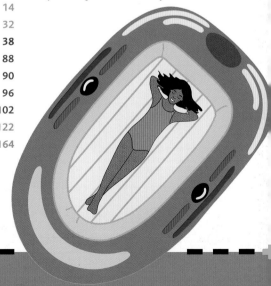

BACK-OF-THE-BOOK QUIZ

Good Luck!

The answers to all the following questions can be found somewhere in London Unlocked. Email a correct set of answers to us and you'll have a chance to win a signed and framed illustration of your choice from the book!

1 How many hours would it take a mole to dig a tunnel as long as the Greenwich Foot Tunnel?

2 Why was Big Ben delayed in 1949?

3 What was the name of the street on which the Great Fire of London broke out?

4 Where is the official central point of London?

5 Where in London can you find a carved human nose inside an arch?

6 How many tonnes of horse poo used to be dropped on the streets of London every day before cars were invented?

A. 100 tonnes
B. 1,000 tonnes
C. 10,000 tonnes

7 What happened to a sparrow at Lord's in 1936?

A. It flew down and ate the King's picnic
B. It got hit by a cricket ball
C. It laid an egg by the cricket stumps

8 Approximately what fraction of the calls the London Fire Brigade get each year are about fires?

A. Three quarters
B. Half
C. One quarter

9 What did Samuel Pepys rescue from the Great Fire of London?

A. His cheese
B. His dressing-gown
C. His cat

10 Which number is the closest to the number of letter As engraved in the banisters and stonework of the Royal Albert Hall?

A. 879
B. 5,456
C. 13,509

Tie-breaker

In no more than 30 words, tell us what is your favourite place in the book and why.

Send your answers to **quiz@unlockedguides.com**

Full terms and conditions are on our website

CENTRAL
NORTH
SOUTH & EAST
WEST
GREENWICH
AROUND
ACROSS
TOP FIVES

CREDITS

Series Editors: Joshua Perry, Emily Kerr
Design: Steve Wells, Allison Curtis, Janice Man
Cartography: Janice Man

Thank you to . . .

Penny Madden for being our Simon Cowell (in a good way). Emma Madden for being our Cheryl Cole. Barry Cunningham for the no nonsense advice. Anne Taute for teaching us how to bluff our way in publishing. Phil Radcliff for being our business guru. Kardy for the dinosaurs, penguins and good humour. Charlotte Coulais for being a huge part of the journey. Sinéad O' Perry for proofreading, patience and all-round loveliness. Johnny Morton, for proofing and patience. Admas Habteslasie for fun site visits and photos. Andy Aicheson for fabulous photos and advice. Joe Craig for words of wisdom on how to write. All our wonderful flickr photographers for making their photos available. You for bothering to read these thankyous (and for buying this book). Steve Wells for getting the format right. Allison Curtis for adding the magic. Janice Man for her level-headed design talent. Hazel, Steve, Tony, Caye, Carla and Ian for loaning us money (we are *sooo* grateful). Bristol Grammar School for allowing us to meet. Hannah Perry for being our company secretary even though we're not entirely sure what that means. The kids at Fox School for their fantastic feedback, especially Aidan, Cole, Emilia, Gabi, James, Joseph, Josie, Louisa, Natalie, Nina, Noah and Sophia. Ruth Knowles for encouraging us to use exclamation marks!!! Red squirrels for their all-round cuteness. Carol Farley for knowing everything there is to know about publicising a travel book. Jess Fawcett for giving us free books and putting us in touch with people.

Finally, thanks to everyone who gave us free and invaluable advice along the way: Amy Cooper, Amy Weaver, Andy Cockburn, Charlie Astor, Chris Dark, Claire Tonks, Colly Myers, George Robinson, all the Kerrs, Laura Bates, Laura Cummings, Lea Lazaric, Luci Heyn, Michael Webster, Nadine Sanders, Natalie Abrahami, Nikki Gamble, Nitya Bolam, Paul Murphy, all the Perrys, Peter Phillipson, Richard North, Rick Edwards, Simon Sporborg, Sophie Fitton, Stella Gurney, Steve Edwards, Tessa Girvan, Toby Sawday, Xenia Hohenlohe . . . *Phew*! As you can see, it was, umm, entirely our own effort.

Oh, and thanks to anyone else we've forgotten.

Photo Credits